The Market Imperative

REFORMING HIGHER EDUCATION:
INNOVATION AND THE PUBLIC GOOD
William G. Tierney and Laura W. Perna, Series Editors

The Market Imperative

Segmentation and Change in Higher Education

Robert Zemsky and Susan Shaman

JOHNS HOPKINS UNIVERSITY PRESS   BALTIMORE

© 2017 Johns Hopkins University Press
All rights reserved. Published 2017
Printed in the United States of America on acid-free paper
9 8 7 6 5 4 3 2 1

Johns Hopkins University Press
2715 North Charles Street
Baltimore, Maryland 21218-4363
www.press.jhu.edu

Library of Congress Cataloging-in-Publication Data

Names: Zemsky, Robert, 1940–, author. | Shaman, Susan, author.
Title: The market imperative : segmentation and change in higher education /
    Robert Zemsky and Susan Shaman.
Description: Baltimore, Maryland : Johns Hopkins University Press, 2017. |
    Series: Reforming higher education: innovation and the public good |
    Includes bibliographical references and index.
Identifiers: LCCN 2017009945| ISBN 9781421424118 (hardcover) | ISBN
    9781421424125 (electronic) | ISBN 1421424118 (hardcover) | ISBN
    1421424126 (electronic)
Subjects: LCSH: Education, Higher—Economic aspects—United States. |
    Universities and colleges—Economic aspects—United States. | Universities
    and colleges—United States—Administration. | Business and education—
    United States. | BISAC: EDUCATION / Higher. | BUSINESS & ECONOMICS /
    Education. | EDUCATION / Educational Policy & Reform / General.
Classification: LCC LC67.62 .Z46 2017 | DDC 378.1/010973—dc23
    LC record available at https://lccn.loc.gov/2017009945

A catalog record for this book is available from the British Library.

*Special discounts are available for bulk purchases of this book. For more information, please
contact Special Sales at 410-516-6936 or specialsales@press.jhu.edu.*

Johns Hopkins University Press uses environmentally friendly book materials,
including recycled text paper that is composed of at least 30 percent post-consumer
waste, whenever possible.

For our always supportive
and patient spouses,
Ann and Paul

Contents

Acknowledgments

As always, our debts to our colleagues and others loom large. Richard Morgan and Gregory Wegner had the unenviable task of editing what we have written in such a way that we took their suggestions as often as possible. Laura Perna played three roles in the birth of this volume—as a consultant to the research team, as an editor of the Johns Hopkins University Press series in which this volume appears, and as an expert on and advocate for state-level higher education policies. As such, she was an early canary in the coal mine of our analysis. Elise Miller, formerly with the Bill & Melinda Gates Foundation, brought us the invitation to revisit our earlier work on the structure of the admissions market and, as a former head of the US Department of Education's Integrated Postsecondary Education Data System, frequently pointed us in the right direction.

Peter Cappelli of the Wharton School at the University of Pennsylvania helped us shape our analysis of what are often conflicting data as to the employability of college graduates at jobs requiring a college education. Sandy Baum's advice helped frame our discussion of federal student aid policy and its impact on the institutions that this book is about. Mark Putnam, president of Iowa's Central College shared with us his understanding of how state actions impacted colleges like his. Two of our executive doctorate students—Becci Menghini, then of the University of Wisconsin–Madison, and Stephen Moret, then of the LSU Foundation—provided important verifications of aspects of our storytelling. Ann Duffield's fingerprints are all over this manuscript, though neither she nor any of our friends, colleagues, or graduate students, to whom we are indebted, are responsible for either our errors or our opinions. Greg Britton of Johns Hopkins University Press was responsible for the final transformation of our manuscript into the finished product you now have before you. We are grateful to Kathleen Capels for her care in shepherding the manuscript through the editorial process. Pamela Erney was the minder who kept us on track.

We thank you all.

The Market Imperative

Prologue

We finished this book on the eve of Donald Trump's inauguration as the nation's forty-fifth president. Like the rest of those involved in American higher education, we duly noted the lamentations and warnings that what would lie ahead for the nation's colleges and universities was more disruption, wrapped in the rhetoric of acrimony and uncertainty. Our take on that moment, however, was somewhat different. First, we were struck by David Gergen's comments following Trump's first and only session with the press prior to his inauguration: "What is now clear is that for all his strengths, Trump is bringing to the White House one of the most combative, intemperate personalities we have ever known. The press conference shows he ain't changing" (Gergen 2017). Then, on reflection, we concluded that what worried us as much was not an uncertain, even toxic future, but rather an immediate past in which drift and listlessness had come to characterize the higher education enterprise.

What did and does trouble us about this moment in time is the increase in student debt; graduation rates that are too low; and discounting practices, particularly among mid-market private colleges and universities, that defy logic. There remains a persistent belief that what is lacking is better consumer data, even though the market has been flooded with consumer report cards of unending variety and little impact. It is a world in which the richest institutions have become ever more aggrandizing, actively recruiting 10 or more applicants for each available place in their first-year classes. The past two decades have witnessed the emergence of for-profit colleges and universities that first enjoyed the largess of federal funding and then the pain of punitive federal regulation, leaving those institutions wounded and their students uncertain as to the value of these schools. There has been a misunderstanding of the role a college education plays in the labor market and, hence, of the value and durability of this education. More generally, the nation's colleges and universities are now viewed with greater skepticism as to their worth and their commitment to the public good.

The problem is that too many of those responsible for the nation's colleges and universities—institutional leaders as well as the makers of public policy—still do not understand just how much the markets they have promoted have changed what American higher education is all about. For more than 30 years, we have made it our business to provide the tools for mapping that territory. Our first foray into this terrain was in the 1980s, when we noted that college and university presidents were more right than they realized when comparing what their institutions charged students for an undergraduate education to what a person would pay for a new car. Colleges and universities, we found, had begun pricing their products in terms of sticker, discount, and cash prices. The first was the stated tuition the institution listed in its catalog and recruiting pieces. The discount price was the sticker price minus any financial aid the institution awarded to the student. And the cash price reflected that student and parental loans were replacing family savings as a principal means of paying for a college education (Shaman and Zemsky 1984).

Next, we produced a structural map of the US market for an undergraduate education that consisted of just three, only slightly overlapping markets—local, regional, and national—in which different kinds of students shopped in each as they went about the business of choosing a college or university. In the late 1990s, we expanded that mapping and, in the process, demonstrated that our classification of markets—now relabeled Medallion, Name Brand, Good Buy, Good Opportunity, and Convenience—predicted the prices institutions could charge. What we demonstrated was that the contours of the market, more than institutional costs, determined the amount charged by these schools. Colleges and universities could not raise all the money they wanted—and thus were limited only to the funds their position in an increasingly competitive market for undergraduate admissions would allow.

More recently, we were asked by the Bill & Melinda Gates Foundation if we thought it possible to replicate our 1997 analysis, which laid out the segment and sector structure that determined the prices most undergraduates paid for their college educations. We thought we could, and we set to work extracting the necessary data. What surprised us most was that the market had become even more segmented and, in that sense, more rigid and dysfunctional. The longer we worked through the data, the more we came to see that the market segment in which a college or university competed shaped that institution's student profile, those students' likely success in an increasingly tough job market, the deployment of faculty assets, the probability of experimenting with distance education, and, as before, the pricing of their products to take advantage of a much-expanded pool of federal financial aid funds.

The most disheartening conclusion we drew from our analyses was that most of the nation's policy makers—at both the federal and state levels—did not understand the market's varying impact on the different kinds of institutions for which these individuals were responsible. As a result, there has been a steady flow of policies that failed to make the sought-after differences or, worse, were responsible for unintended consequences that turned out to be real disasters. The government's decision to make federally funded student aid available to those enrolled at for-profit institutions was a prime example of where reverberations are still being felt—in terms of unreasonably high student debt levels, on the one hand, and, on the other, a culture of fraud and customer abuse that today has led to a host of contentious institutional closures.

Periodically, our colleague Greg Wegner would ask, "Who is the audience for your work?" Our answer was that we wanted to reach those responsible for governmental policies and institutional practices—those for whom not knowing the territory, not understanding the dynamics of the market, was truly dangerous. But we also wanted to reach out to all those interested in, committed to, or simply angry with the nation's colleges and universities.

Thus, our volume has three purposes. First, to describe the structure of the market for undergraduate education in terms of its sectors and segments, as well as the role those elements play in shaping student lives and institutional contexts. Second, to use what we learned about the structure of the market to explain the composition of an American higher education enterprise that today comprises roughly 4,000 separate institutions and around 17.3 million undergraduates, or "customers," annually. As before, we wanted to analyze how and why institutions charged different prices. Just as importantly, we wanted to demonstrate how the same forces that established price also determined the composition and nature of the faculty, the kinds of courses and programs they were likely to offer, and the success individual students probably would achieve at different kinds of institutions.

These first two purposes determined the organization of the volume you are about to read. We begin with a detailed examination of the market prices the nation's colleges and universities now charge and present a variety of models demonstrating the role graduation rates and discounting practices play in determining the price for an undergraduate education at a baccalaureate institution. For America's community colleges, we show the parallel role played by degree focus—the extent to which those colleges were in the business of granting associate degrees. Chapter 1 charts the very real differences between and among the market's segments and the result that, most often, institutional differences are minimalized among those in the same market segment. In chapter 2, we summarize the basic demographic and institutional characteristics revealed by our market-segment modeling. Chapter 3 looks at student consumers and the roles market or consumer information can and cannot play in promoting changes in institutional practices. Chapter 4 seeks to understand how and why it has proven so easy for colleges and universities to promise more than they can deliver in terms of good, sustainable jobs for their graduates. In chapter 5, we chart how markets differ between and among the 50 states. Chapter 6 focuses on faculty and how the markets distribute different kinds of faculty across higher education's principal segments. Chapter 7 is our summary mapping of the territory that needs to be better understood if American higher education is going to change.

Third, our most audacious goal, no doubt, is our attempt to explain to those most responsible for both state and federal higher education policy that they are making a muck of the enterprise. You do not need to read to the end of this volume to learn that we came to regard former president Barack Obama's failed proposal to rate the nation's colleges and universities in terms of their economic and educational efficiency—the former measured by the prices they charge and the latter by their ability to hold on to their students through graduation—as not just wrong-headed, but actually dangerous. The push for metrics and for ways of ensuring that graduates are gainfully employed upon graduation now poses the same kind of danger, in large part because too many of those who focus on jobs and employability do not understand the consequences of a global labor market that is becoming saturated with college graduates. And just to make sure we have left no feathers unruffled, we point out that state-level policy making has all but disappeared, having become the victim of weak imaginations, insufficient funding, and an aversion to targeted investment.

We conclude with an epilogue, presenting four basic propositions for changing higher education. The first is to recapture the interests and talents of the faculty in the process of institutional reform. Here we confront a conundrum. Faculty mostly see themselves as the victims of the market forces and related miscalculations that have reshaped the world of the academy. Their response to these changes has been to preserve their independence, so they can continue to teach "their students" and do "their research," while leaving the messy business of responding to societal changes to others. What their institutions need, however, is a truly collective commitment to change that only an energized as well as an empowered faculty can deliver.

Our second proposition should surprise no one. What the nation needs now is a cohort of federal and state policy makers who understand the markets their policies have largely created, the ways in which those markets distribute students and faculty, the kinds of educational programs they promote, and their varying impact on the labor market.

Third, it is past the time to rethink how the federal government financially promotes educational access and attainment. An experiment that began in the 1960s, with federal aid going to students, rather than directly to institutions, has run its course. Now what is needed is direct investment, in the form of operating subsidies designed to achieve the goals of federal policy. We believe, for example, that the objective of improving the education offered by the nation's community colleges would be much better served by providing monies directly to these institutions, rather than funding an additional federal student aid program.

Fourth, we argue that it is time to stop overpromising higher education's capacity to spur economic growth. Our read on the history of the last 40 years is that higher education has prospered most often when the nation's economy is expanding, and only very rarely can colleges and universities be said to promote general economic growth.

That leaves the question of what the current federal administration intends. What we don't recommend is a period of benign neglect, though, no doubt, that is what many within higher education believe is the best they can hope for. Leaving higher education alone, however, would mean more of the same—more drift; more federal student aid programs riddled with unintended consequences that benefit almost no one; and more largely ineffective jawboning about the need to reduce student debt and curb colleges' appetites for price increases, particularly among publicly funded institutions. What is needed instead is a willingness to rethink the basic assumptions that have governed federal higher education policy for the past three-plus decades. And only a rich and robust national conversation about the purposes of a college education is likely to produce the recasting that is now overdue. It is, however, anyone's guess whether the current president, or his party, or his opposition, has any interest in convening such a conversation.

1

Market Price

As the Walrus in Lewis Carroll's *Through the Looking Glass* knew, it is the sorting out that matters most. In the pages that follow, we have used data drawn from the US Department of Education's Integrated Postsecondary Education Data System (IPEDS) to map American colleges and universities into recognizable clusters, or segments, that facilitate the making of comparisons within groups of similar institutions. We have also constructed a set of indices, or measures, that document the performance of these institutions in terms of access and completions. To accomplish this latter task, we wanted to be able to describe each institution's undergraduate student body along four gauges of diversity: economic, race and ethnicity, age, and geography. What we have sought, then, is a taxonomy that fully reflects the nature of American higher education today. Because we are interested in the role the market has played in shaping—and not just occasionally thwarting—important educational reforms, we have looked for a way of depicting the structure of that market and its impacts on consumer behavior, institutional strategies, and public policies. To begin that process, in this chapter we present a set of market taxonomies that help predict and, in that sense, help explain the market prices differing institutions charge.

A Taxonomic Challenge

Though not an overly familiar term when applied to higher education, taxonomies for sorting American colleges and universities abound—and have done so for more than a century. By the middle of the twentieth century, the often parochial nature of these groupings had spawned two major attempts to develop a classification system that was more inclusive, while, at the same time, taking note of the basic diversity of American higher education. The first was a grouping of institutions using just two variables: control (public or private), and the nature of the degrees provided and the prescribed length of time it took a student to earn a degree. The resulting classification produced three basic groups: two-year schools; four-year colleges and universities; and those offering graduate degrees, advanced professional degrees, or both.

About the same time that this control/principal degree classification was becoming familiar to consumers and policy makers, the Carnegie Commission on Higher Education developed an alternative, more robust way of categorizing the nation's system of higher education. What came to be known in 1971 as the Carnegie Classification and the Carnegie Categories reflected the interests and experiences of Clark Kerr, former president of the University of California System, and the 1960 California Master Plan for Higher Education, for which he was largely responsible. What the Carnegie Classification added to the political taxonomy then holding sway was a keen sense of mission differentiation (McCormick and Zhao 2005).

Thirty years later, time and circumstance had eroded the broad acceptance of Kerr's original scheme—slightly revised over time—and the parallel political taxonomy that grouped colleges and universities in terms of their institutional control. The world, it turned out, had grown both more complex and competitively quarrelsome. By then, a burgeoning sector of for-profit institutions already accounted for upward of 10 percent of all postsecondary enrollments; public four-year colleges had all but disappeared, as nearly every institution wanted to be known as a university; in growing numbers, public two-year colleges were beginning to offer specialized baccalaureate degrees; and private two-year institutions— the original junior colleges that once flourished nearly everywhere—had either closed or morphed into four-year institutions. There was a growing sense that, on the one hand, the reigning Carnegie Classification cataloged elements that were no longer the most important and, on the other, it fostered a competition among colleges and universities that was leading US higher education in the wrong direction—making research more important than teaching and encouraging a kind of incipient mission creep among almost all institutions not already renowned for their wealth and research prowess.

One of the first taxonomies to challenge the old order was developed by our team at the University of Pennsylvania's Institute for Research on Higher Education (IRHE), as part of a larger College Board effort to launch its Enrollment Planning Service. The modeling we performed for this effort focused not on institutions, but on students, assigning each individual to one of three broad categories, based on the distribution of the colleges and universities to which they sent their SAT scores. We learned that most students shopped in only one sphere—national, regional, or local—and schools could be characterized by their dominant applicant populations (again, as national, regional, or local institutions). What distinguished the Enrollment Planning Service's approach to classifying US higher education was its use of a market perspective to group colleges and universities, rather than either institutional mission or legal status (Zemsky and Oedel 1983).

In the mid-1990s, the IRHE team returned to the fray, this time persuaded that the higher education market was more than a convenient metaphor for explaining the competition for undergraduate enrollments. Now working as part of the US Department of Education's National Center for Postsecondary Improvement (NCPI), we constructed a new market taxonomy that predicted market behavior in general and, in particular, the prices institutions charged. Somewhat to our surprise, the resulting market models explained nearly 60 percent of the variance among the prices that private, four-year institutions were charging. In all, the NCPI's market taxonomy was limited to just a handful of variables: region, admit (i.e., admission) rate, yield, and five-year graduation rate. The underlying model was less successful in predicting prices at public institutions, though it, too, yielded a set of definable market segments with relatively homogenous prices. The conclusion we came to then—erroneously, we now believe—was that in the public sector of higher education, the prices students paid were more a function of political and policy considerations than the value the market had assigned to each institution competing for undergraduate enrollments.

From this work, we developed our general definition of a market taxonomy: a construct that maps the contours of the higher education admissions market in terms of the prices students and families pay to attend the college or university of their choice, and shows how clusters of institutions differ from one another in terms of the students they attract (including their racial and economic diversity and geographic location), the scope of their programs, and (not to be forgotten) the probability that students attending a particular institution would graduate with a baccalaureate degree in a reasonable period of time. The NCPI taxonomy, initially presented in *Change* (1998) and later more fully documented in *Higher Education as Competitive Enterprise: When Markets Matter* (Zemsky, Shaman, and Shapiro 2001), comprised the five institutional types that continue to frame our market analyses today.

— *Medallion*: a segment that includes the nation's most competitive institutions and students, for which prestige-based rankings, such as those annually published by *US News & World Report*, have played an ever-increasing role in defining institutional ambitions and, hence, quality.

— *Name Brand*: a segment largely populated by well-known institutions. Most practice selective admissions, though their appeal is more likely to be regional than national. Many, but not all, of these institutions would like to be Medallions.

— *Good Buy*: a segment comprising a variety of institutions, for the most part offering full-scale undergraduate programs at prices substantially less than those of institutions practicing selective admissions.

— *Good Opportunity*: a segment consisting of institutions and students who see higher education as a special possibility. Many students who shop in this segment are the first in their families to attend college.

— *Convenience (user-friendly)*: the one segment in which part-time as well as intermittent learners dominate. Its students often shop for a friendly environment at an institution that understands their special requirements, including the need to take courses at convenient times.

Calculating Average Market Price

Our new analysis begins with a more nuanced way of defining an average, or mean, market price for each of the four sectors. For each student—in our analysis, freshmen, as a proxy for all undergraduates—the market price is the stated amount of tuition minus his or her institutional financial aid award. Each institution's average market price is the sum of the market prices for all its first-time, full-time freshmen divided by the number of freshmen. The mean, or average, market price in a set—say, a sector—is the sum of the institutional average market prices divided by the number of institutions in the set. Here it is important to note that a college or university's average market price is different from and is always higher than the average net price a student pays, unless every student pays the full, or sticker, price that institution lists in its publications. Most commentators and policy makers have focused on the average net price to the student—and schools are required by federal mandate to include a "net price calculator" on their websites. From market and institutional perspectives, however, the more cogent and important calculation is the mean market price, which, according to our definition, is the average amount of cash the institution receives from its enrolled undergraduate students. Net price reflects the availability of both institutional and external sources of aid, such as Pell Grants, other federal grants, scholarships, and subsidies, along with state grants-in-aid and externally funded scholarships. Market price (sometimes dubbed the discounted price), as we have defined it, reflects how the market values a particular institution.

The easiest way to describe the difference between net price and market, or discounted, price is to note that the latter allows an institution to focus on its actual revenues, while the former draws attention to how individual students pay for their college education. While it is possible to arrive at a school's average market price using data from IPEDS, the average net price its students pay cannot be similarly calculated, because it is not possible to know how much external—as opposed to institutional—aid its students receive.

As in our earlier analyses, relatively few variables were needed to develop a credible model for estimating the average market price for individual institutions. Although we created more fully explanatory models for the four-year market, we found that we could produce a reasonable estimate of a college or university's average market price using only its six-year (or equivalent) graduation rate for full-time students—a measure that has little, if any, relevance for either the two-year or the transfer market (table 1.1).

We next tested whether the market within a given sector was composed of separate segments—as was the case through at least the year 2000. In practical terms, we needed to ask whether knowing an institution's

Table 1.1. Predicting market price from graduation rates

Sector	Correlation coefficient of graduation rate vs. market price	Mean market price ($)	Mean graduation rate (%)	Estimated change in market price for each percentage change in graduation rate ($)
Private Not-for-Profit	0.611	15,060	57.3	188
Public Four-Year	0.581	7,434	48.7	112
Private For-Profit	0.625	13,665	25.5	153

Note: It is our convention to use correlation (*r*) to measure association in a two-variable relationship and *R*-squared to measure the model's explanatory power in multivariable models.

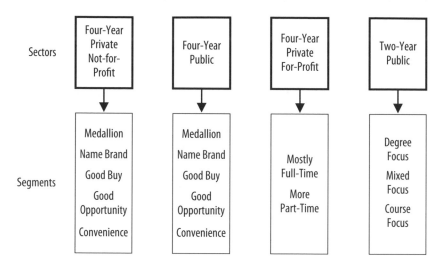

Figure 1.1. Market segments within sectors

market segment yielded a more accurate estimate of its market price than the average price for its particular sector. (The taxonomy of sector and segment is illustrated in the schematic in figure 1.1.) We divided the Four-Year Private Not-for-Profit and Four-Year Public sectors into their relevant market segments, based on each institution's six-year (or equivalent) graduation rate, and again used the terminology developed earlier: Medallion, Name Brand, Good Buy, Good Opportunity, and Convenience institutions. Later in this chapter, we will discuss the For-Profit and the Two-Year Public sectors.

Table 1.2. Market segment regression model: Four-Year Private
Not-for-Profit sector, salient variables

Segment	Number	Regression R-squared	Mean market price ($)	Mean discount rate (%)
Medallion	119	0.688	23,695	40
Name Brand	148	0.696	16,870	46
Good Buy	330	0.525	14,190	53
Good Opportunity	294	0.360	12,434	39
Convenience	89	results not significant	11,677	34

Note: It is our convention to use correlation (*r*) to measure association in a two-variable re-lationship and *R*-squared to measure the model's explanatory power in multivariable models.

The Four-Year Private Not-for-Profit Sector

The explanatory power of this segmenting is best reflected in the results for the Four-Year Private Not-for-Profit sector. Table 1.2 displays summary results, showing that the average market price decreases monotonically across the sector, from the Medallion through Convenience segments. Each model's fit (*R*-squared) follows the same pattern: strongest among the highly competitive Medallion and Name Brand segments. The Medallion segment includes such institutions as Harvard, Georgetown, and Rice Universities, and Wesleyan, Pomona, and Grinnell Colleges. The Name Brand segment includes Case Western Reserve and Southern Methodist Universities, as well as Earlham, Washington & Jefferson, and Ithaca Colleges. Within the Convenience segment, on the other hand, the model is much weaker, having neither predictive nor explanatory power. The discount rates reflect something of the near desperation in the middle of this sector, with Four-Year Private institutions of every description trying to find a tuition point that yields both revenue and students, rather than just one or the other.

The independent variables in these models illuminate some of the important relationships that undergird the setting of tuition rates. Some are expected, and others are not. For example, within the Medallion segment, the admit rate is not a significant predictor of price, since practically all of these institutions have large, surplus applicant pools. Yield rate, however, is significant, and negative. Since almost all of the schools in this segment practice a form of need-blind admissions, with assistance often paid for by generous endowment funds, the more students a college or university can afford to help monetarily, the lower the average market price. It also follows that the greater the ratio of institutional aid to other forms of grants, the lower the market price. But this relationship is limited to those schools that, for the most part, use their aid budgets to meet demonstrated need, rather than discounting their prices to ensure a larger class of first-time students.

The Name Brand segment differs from the Medallion one in two important ways. First, both graduation and admit rates are important predictors of average market price within the former but not the latter, suggesting that the Name Brand segment is competitively much less homogeneous. At the same time, specialization, as reflected in the percentage of students in an institution's largest major, predicts an increase in the average market price in the Name Brand but not the Medallion segment.

The Four-Year Public Sector

We turn next to the Four-Year Public sector, somewhat smaller in terms of number of institutions, but dramatically larger in terms of the proportion of undergraduate enrollments: two-thirds of all baccalaureate (or equivalent) enrollments, and one-third of all degree-seeking undergraduate enrollments. The largest are the sector's mega-flagships, led by Arizona State, at 58,184 degree-seeking undergraduates; Central Florida, with 49,559; and Ohio State, with 41,709. In 2012, there were 19 universities with undergraduate enrollments of 30,000 or more—a set of institutions that reads like the roster for big-time college sports. There were also more small schools than might have been expected: 134, or nearly a quarter of the four-year public colleges and universities in our study had enrollments of less than 3,000 undergraduates, though most of these were branch campuses of a large Public flagship university. The median size for the segment (the enrollment number in the middle of set, for which half of the enrollments were larger and half were smaller) was 6,959 undergraduates, and the mean was 10,025.

Table 1.3 reports the average amount of institutional aid per undergraduate, the mean market price, and the percentage of degree-seeking undergraduates who attend part time. Compared with the average market prices charged by Four-Year Private Not-for-Profit institutions, those in the Four-Year Public sector were both lower and more tightly bunched. The mean and median average market prices in this sector in 2011–12 were

Table 1.3. Market segment profile: Four-Year Public Sector, salient variables

Segment	Number	Mean part-time degree-seekers (%)	Mean market price ($)	Mean institutional grant aid per full-time, first-time undergraduate ($)
Medallion	25	3	12,883	7,403
Name Brand	70	7	9,928	5,222
Good Buy	249	14	7,388	3,940
Good Opportunity	117	19	5,771	3,760
Convenience	30	46	5,520	3,144

$7,397 and $6,694, respectively. The highest average market price was $19,521, charged by the University of Vermont, closely followed by $19,490 at the Pennsylvania State University's main campus.

As in the Four-Year Private Not-for-Profit sector, average market prices in the Four-Year Public sector tracked graduation rates. On the other hand, average market prices in this Public sector were not quite as amenable to modeling as the average market prices in the Four-Year Private Not-for-Profit sector. Using the same set of independent variables to predict average market price used in the Private models, we could explain just under half, as opposed to just under two-thirds, of the variation in average market price. As in the Four-Year Private Not-for-Profit sector, the key variables for estimating an institution's market price were its graduation rate, its admit rate, the size of its undergraduate student body, and the size of its entering class. The most important difference separating the Four-Year Public and the Four-Year Private Not-for-Profit sectors, however, was the absence of the two key financial aid variables from the list of significant independent variables for public colleges and universities: the percentage of undergraduates receiving financial aid, and the ratio of institutional aid to all financial aid. Our hypothesis is that this result is a function both of the smaller role financial aid plays in public institutions, as compared with private ones—an important attribute shoppers should keep in mind when choosing where to enroll—and the often idiosyncratic part played by differing state financial aid policies.

The list of the 25 Medallion Four-Year Public institutions in the United States corresponds remarkably well to the public's notion of Public flagship institutions: the six University of California campuses; the Universities of Michigan, Virginia, and Illinois; the Pennsylvania State University; plus a small number of non–Association of American Universities (AAU) institutions, such as James Madison University in Virginia, the College of New Jersey, and St. Mary's College of Maryland. The Convenience segment had too few institutions with complete data—just 30 in all—so that segment was not included in our analysis of the Four-Year Public market segments.

The ordered structure of the Four-Year Public sector market segment, like that of the Four-Year Private Not-for-Profit sector, is reflected in the decreasing values of market price and institutional grants and, in the case of the percentage of degree-seeking undergraduates who attend part time, the increasing values from the Medallion through Convenience segments. What mattered most in the Medallion / Name Brand competition for students prepared to pay an above-average market price was a college or university's six-year or equivalent graduation rate (essentially a proxy for prestige) and the availability of institutional aid—two characteristics common among all highly competitive four-year institutions, whether they are Public or Private Not-for-Profits.

The competitive fault lines that gave shape to the American market for undergraduate education more than two decades ago continue to do so now, though their consequences are felt more strongly, particularly among the nation's less competitive Private Not-for-Profit institutions, which are now caught up in a frenzy of discounting that generates sufficient enrollments but inadequate revenues.

The Four-Year Private For-Profit Sector

The biggest change overall is the emergence of a Four-Year Private For-Profit sector, now enrolling more than one out of every ten students seeking an undergraduate degree. On average, 80 percent of the degrees awarded by those institutions are bachelor's degrees. Developing a workable average market price model for the Four-Year Private For-Profit sector was not without its challenges. It is a sector dominated by a handful of big, powerful, for-profit enterprises that are networks of linked locations, rather than separate campuses, although their data are stored in IPEDS as though they were separate entities. For modeling purposes, we abided by the IPEDS convention of treating each entity as a separate campus/ institution. In the data we analyzed, there were 66 separate Universities of

Phoenix entities, 21 Art Institutes, 26 DeVry Universities (including one DeVry College), and so on. At the same time, this sector is inordinately dependent on federal student aid, in the form of both Pell Grants and federally managed student loans—a circumstance we believe further confounds our data problems. There is, for example, a persistent belief across the for-profit sector that the federal government's 90:10 rule—the requirement that at least 10 percent of revenues received from students come from a source other than the federal government, including Title IV and non–Title IV funds—compels some institutions to raise their prices, in order to absorb all available federal student aid and still generate their required additional revenue.

In terms of our market pricing models, the For-Profit sector was remarkably well behaved. For the 72 percent of the institutions among the 254 in our final data set that reported the percentage of their students who graduated with a baccalaureate degree within six years (or equivalent) of their initial enrollment, the same basic relationship between graduation rates and average market prices holds: as graduation rates increase, so do average market prices. At the same time, the graduation rates (when reported) were low, generally 50 percent or less.

While, as required, all institutions in this sector reported completions, more than 40 percent of the ones with large part-time enrollments did not report six-year (or equivalent) graduation rates. Hence we could not use graduation rates to segment this sector. Nor, as it turned out, could we use the other two principal variables we used in the Four-Year Public or the Four-Year Private Not-for-Profit models: admit and yield rates. In the end, we partitioned this sector by the proportion of an institution's enrollment that was comprised of part-time students. The result was a For-Profit sector with just two segments: those Four-Year Private For-Profit schools with more than a third of their students attending part time (i.e., More Part-Time); and those with less than a third of their students attending part time (i.e., Mostly Full-Time).

Less than half of the for-profit baccalaureate institutions in our IPEDS data set report admit or yield rates—a not surprising result, given that almost all For-Profit colleges and universities are open-enrollment institutions that neither collect nor pay much attention to admit or yield rates. One explanatory variable that tracked well with an institution's market

Table 1.4. Predicting market price from percentage of students age 30 or older

Sector	Correlation coefficient of age 30+ vs. market price	Mean market price ($)	Mean percentage age 30+	Change in market price ($) for each percentage change in age 30+
Private For-Profit	0.609	13,691	44	−110

Note: It is our convention to use correlation (*r*) to measure association in a two-variable relationship and R-squared to measure the model's explanatory power in multivariable models.

price was the percentage of undergraduates who were 30 or more years old. More than half the For-Profit baccalaureate colleges and universities reported that over 50 percent of their students were in this age bracket. The higher the proportion of students who are 30-plus years old, the lower the average market price (table 1.4).

For the Mostly Full-Time set of institutions, constituting over half of the Four-Year Private For-Profit sector, the basic model predicting average market price works remarkably well, explaining just over 70 percent of the variance—a result that matches those for the Medallion Not-for-Profit segment. There is substantially less predictive power in the model when applied to the More Part-Time segment of the Four-Year Private For-Profit sector, accounting for just 37 percent of the variance in average market price.

Our overall model explained just over half (53 percent) of the variance in prices across the sector—a more than respectable result, covering roughly the same portion of price variance as did our model for the Four-Year Public sector. Some of the findings reflected in the model have already been highlighted, such as the greater the proportion of an institution's undergraduate population 30 years of age or older, the lower the average market price. On the other hand, and probably a sustaining reflection of the For-Profit sector's early history, the more specialized a college or university's offerings, the higher its average market price. Institutions more attractive to students with Pell Grants have slightly lower market prices. As in the Four-Year Public and Private Not-for-Profit sectors, segmenting the For-Profit market substantially improves our ability to estimate average market prices.

The Two-Year Public Sector

Fifteen years ago, the single largest sector of American higher education was composed of the institutions IPEDS classified as Two-Year Public—though increasing numbers of those schools were morphing into four-year colleges, offering a limited number of specialized and vocational baccalaureate degrees. While the Four-Year Public sector has overtaken the Two-Year one in enrollments—6.8 million versus 6.4 million in 2014—the Two-Year Public sector remains a large and crucial part of the higher education landscape. Although no single independent variable could be regarded as a principal estimator of average market prices across the Two-Year Public sector—as the graduation rate is in the Four-Year Public and Not-for-Profit sectors, and the percentage of part-time students is in the Four-Year For-Profit sector—it was still possible to define a pricing model that explained much of the variation in average market prices.

In one important way, the best model for estimating average market prices runs counter to the models for estimating prices in the For-Profit sector. Here, the higher the percentage of part-time degree seekers, the lower the average market price. The most striking difference, however, is in the role played by geography and regional history. In the areas of the country that first championed lower-cost public community colleges, the Far West and throughout the Sun Belt, two-year institutions charge lower average market prices.

Roughly 15 years ago, we solved the riddle of pricing across community colleges by noting that there were essentially three groups, or clumps, of institutions: those that focused on credentials, those that focused on courses, and institutions that did both. It is a definitional schema that works as well today as it did in 2000. A Two-Year Public college is said to be degree-focused (labeled Degree Focus) if the institution reported that 15 percent or more of its students were either degree or certificate seeking, and less than half of its students were attending part time. For the most part, it is these institutions that center on providing an entry point to a baccalaureate degree to be completed at either a Public or a Private Four-Year institution. Course Focus colleges are defined as those reporting that less than 15 percent of their students were degree or certificate seeking—hence more course focused—and more than half of their enrolled students were attending part time. Mixed Focus institutions were defined as those

Table 1.5. Market segment profile: Two-Year Public sector

Segment	Number	Mean part-time degree seekers (%)	Mean full-time, first-time undergraduates receiving grant aid (%)	Mean market price ($)
Degree Focus	427	34	79	3,318
Mixed Focus	380	54	72	3,096
Course Focus	216	64	66	2,373

that satisfied only one of the key criteria, but not both. In all, we labeled 427 institutions as Degree Focus, 216 as Course Focus, and 380 as Mixed Focus (table 1.5).

When modeled separately, each of these three Two-Year Public segments tells a slightly different story. The model estimating the average market prices of the Course Focus institutions explained more than three-quarters of the price variation in this segment, while the model estimating the average market prices for the Degree Focus institutions accounted for much less of the variation, just 31 percent. As might be expected, the model estimating the average market price of institutions that were neither Degree nor Course Focus fell somewhere in the middle, at 39 percent.

Two cogent differences among the institutions in this segment are worth noting. First, in the model estimating the average market prices of Degree Focus institutions, the higher the retention rate, the higher the average market price, all other things being equal. The opposite was the case in the other two segments: the higher the average market price, the lower the retention rate, again with all other elements being equal. Second, the model estimating average market prices for Course Focus institutions reflects the roles that politics plus geography have played in shaping the pricing practices of Public institutions. Regional effects are strongest in this segment.

For community colleges, the big story is simply that, despite the belief of many, the Two-Year Public market can best be seen as an active extension of the larger market for postsecondary education, rather than as a separate domain governed almost exclusively by local traditions. Community colleges are part of, rather than separate from, the market and are likely to become even more of a factor in the larger national narrative over the coming decade.

Looking Forward

Three more conclusions—harbingers of things to come—are also reflected in our analysis of average market prices. The first is a pervasive feeling that the market for postsecondary education is in the process of splitting into two almost wholly separate markets, and that individual institutions will have to decide which one they wish to compete in. The first part of the market will be composed principally of institutions that seek out—indeed cater to—young, full-time college students. The more traditionally configured the college or university and the more successful its marketing campaigns, the higher its average market price is likely to be. The institutions that cannot compete in this arena will find themselves discounting their sticker prices to the point where they simply do not have enough revenue to cover their operating costs.

The other part of the market most likely will be dominated by institutions that seek out in some combination of 30-plus-year-old learners, part-time students, and students willing to enroll in online learning programs. This part of the market will probably prove to be more cost sensitive, with their average market prices constrained—as is already the case in the For-Profit market—by the ready availability of federal student aid, both as loans and as grants. No doubt traditionally configured colleges and universities, already burdened with high discount rates, will try to augment their usual enrollments by dipping into this "other market." What they may well discover, however, is that for the indefinite future, trying to compete in both the traditional and the spot markets for postsecondary education will prove to be a losing proposition.

Second, at the lower end of the market, there can be a destructive price competition that threatens both quality and the ability to innovate. Not surprisingly, the negative consequences of nearly unconstrained competition, fueled by an ever-increasing demand, has allowed Medallion institutions to become, for all practical purposes, an oligopoly when it comes to setting their own prices.

The third summary conclusion we offer derives from data showing that the colleges and universities with the best records on completion are also those (again, Public as well as Private) with the highest average market prices in their sector—or, conversely, that those institutions with the lowest average market prices almost uniformly have lower completion rates. What the federal government—cheered on by a host of well-funded foundations and increasingly vocal policy wonks—recently had been seeking is an outcome that squares this circle, such that prices can be constrained, if not lowered, and completions simultaneously increased. What our market analysis suggests is that achieving this result will require a major intervention in the market itself, which, in practical terms, will mean a smarter set of federal policies and programs for spending the monies governments, both nationally and in the 50 states, are already investing in support of equal access and opportunity. It is a subject we will return to once we have completed our explorations of the market's mechanics.

2

Sectors and Segments

Today's higher education landscape is dominated by a market that has both sharp edges and critical differences. To describe the roles that sectors and segments play in this shaping of the American undergraduate enterprise, we have developed what might best be called a graphical lexicon—quite literally a graphic vocabulary—for depicting the market challenges likely to face all would-be reformers of undergraduate education, now and in the future. The place to start is with a reprise of our basic finding for the most traditional part of the enterprise: the market price (that is, the average amount of revenue received per undergraduate) for a four-year baccalaureate institution, either a Public or a Private Not-for-Profit, is a function of the sector and segment to which it belongs.

The First Three: Prices, Pell Recipients, and Discounts

The graphs that compose figure 2.1 summarize what we know about the annual pricing of full-time enrollment in a baccalaureate-granting college or university, the distribution of Pell Grants among these undergraduates, and the distribution of institutional grants to first-time, full-time students across these same institutions. The two graphs in figure 2.1 first illustrate the importance of sector with respect to market price (*top*), and then the very different results that can arise through the interplay of sectors and segments on two financial aid measures (*bottom*): the percentage of students receiving institutional aid (i.e., discounts) and the percentage receiving Pell Grants.

The market prices across the segments in the Four-Year Private Not-for-Profit and Public sectors create similar tracks, descending from the

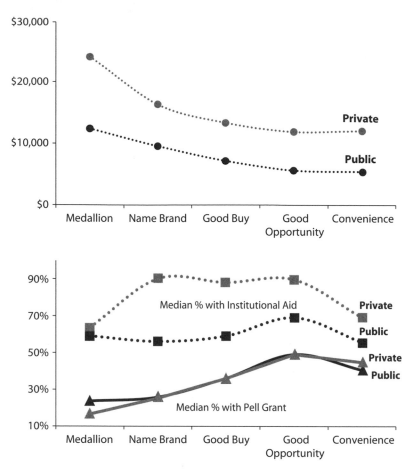

Figure 2.1. Median market prices (*top*) and median percentages with Pell Grant recipients and students with other discounts (*bottom*). *Note*: Public=Four-Year Public; Private=Four-Year Private Not-for-Profit.

Medallion to the Good Opportunity segments, and essentially flattening at the Convenience segment. While there is variance *within* a particular segment, there is minimal overlap in prices *between* segments. For example, among Four-Year Private Not-for-Profit Medallions in 2012, 50 percent of all institutions had annual market prices between $27,620 and $20,566. At $19,661, the 75th percentile of market price in the Name Brand segment fell below the 25th percentile of the Medallions. In the Four-Year Public sector, the price bands were tighter, and there was a bit more overlap between segments.

The curves in the lower graph track the median percentages of Pell Grant and institutional grant recipients in each sector and segment, and they teach another lesson. For Pell recipients—a proxy for lower-income students—the curves with the triangular data points tell us that segment matters a great deal, and sector not at all. The median percentage of Pell recipients in the Private and Public sectors increases monotonically from Medallion through Good Opportunity institutions, and, more importantly, these percentages are identical for the two sectors in the middle three segments. To the extent that the distribution of Pell recipients mirrors the distribution of lower-income students, figure 2.2 supports the argument that advocates for mid-market Private colleges and universities have long made—that their institutions serve the same basic market as mid-market Public colleges and universities.

A third pattern results when the question becomes, "What percentage of undergraduates receive institutional aid?" Here the big difference is between the two sectors (the dotted lines with square data points in figure 2.1). The distribution among the Public institutions presents a fairly uniform pattern, with the percentage of first-time, full-time undergraduates receiving institutional aid wavering modestly from the Medallion through Convenience segments, but peaking at Good Opportunity, essentially reflecting the relatively lower market prices of colleges and universities in that segment. The distribution of institutional aid among the Private Not-for-Profit schools reflects, perhaps, the near panic of less-selective institutions within this sector that have engaged in price discounting, under the guise of offering increased institutional aid. Private Convenience colleges and universities (for the most part open-admissions institutions), on one end of the spectrum have proven to be less frantic in their discounting, while most of the nation's Medallion schools have continued to limit the awarding of institutional aid to those with demonstrated financial need.

The Demography of Access

With these three dominant patterns in mind, we can begin a more detailed exploration of how, when, and why sectors and segments matter—and how those divisions reinforce old prejudices and stereotypes, as well as offering only limited opportunities for changing the demographic realities that shape American higher education. Here we focus on the four

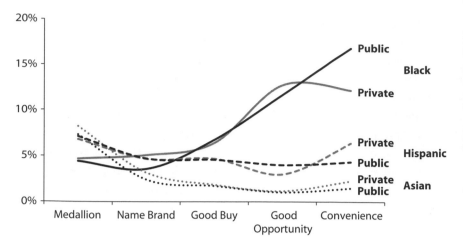

Figure 2.2. Student ethnicity. *Note*: Public=Four-Year Public; Private=Four-Year Private Not-for-Profit.

groups of students often identified in terms of their race or ethnicity and their countries of origin: labeled in the IPEDS database as Hispanic, Black (or as "Black or African American"), Asian, and Nonresident Alien (i.e., international) students. First, we examine students who classify themselves as Hispanic, though in this case the sector/segment alignment explains very little, if anything, about their higher education experience. The dashed lines in figure 2.2 illustrate how and when our graphical lexicon signals less-predictable behavior than we have encountered so far when depicting the structure of the American market for a baccalaureate education. While our analysis did show a more prominent presence of Hispanic students in some Public Convenience institutions—more than a quarter of which reported that at least 20 percent of their students were Hispanic—there is little difference in the distribution of the median percentage of Hispanic students between sectors or across segments (as depicted in the two dashed lines), since the lines do not have a pronounced slope.

Put in policy terms, figure 2.2 teaches two important lessons. First, Hispanic enrollments in baccalaureate institutions remain noticeably low—except, as was observed but not graphed, in a limited number of largely public, Hispanic-serving institutions. Second, from the perspective of trying to understand the structure of the market, figure 2.2 reflects the absence of what might best be called a Hispanic market signature, as well as the near absence of baccalaureate institutions specializing in serving Hispanics' interests. As we note later in this chapter, however, there is a decidedly Hispanic signature in the market for Public community colleges.

In sharp contrast, the two remaining demographic groups that are at the center of most discussions of access and opportunity—Blacks and Asians—have quite discernible market signatures. For Blacks (the solid lines in figure 2.2), that signature begins, reading left to right, with a strong upward shift toward the lower-cost and the Convenience side of the spectrum. Segment is a key factor; sector makes little difference. Our analysis showed that there was substantial dispersion above the median, particularly among Good Opportunity and Convenience institutions, suggesting that Black enrollments have come to be concentrated in a limited number of colleges and universities. The market signature for Asians (the dotted lines in figure 2.2) is the inverse of the one for the African American market—in this case the shift is downward, making Medallion the dominant segment in both the Private Not-for-Profit and the Public sectors. We found that the dispersal about the median in the Public sector is particularly pronounced, with nearly a quarter of the Public Medallion colleges and universities reporting that 20 percent or more of their enrolled undergraduates identify themselves as Asians. The Nonresident Alien student market signature (not included in figure 2.2) mirrors that of the distribution of Hispanic students, except that the numbers for the former are smaller and have a tighter dispersion about the median.

What give rise to these distributions are cultural habits, predilections, and, for some locales, geography. They are neither accidental nor temporary, nor, for that matter, are they easily changed. For example, the lesson learned by those who lament that Black students appear to enroll in less competitive, less selective institutions than their precollegiate preparation would equip them for—what William Bowen, Matthew Chingos, and Michael McPherson (2011) describe as "undermatching"—is that their argument often falls on deaf ears among the leaders in the African American community, particularly those who champion historically Black colleges and universities.

Form and Function

If our market sector / market segment model for baccalaureate education did nothing more than provide a basis for predicting average market prices, it would still represent a substantial analytical achievement. If the model also supplies a greater and more nuanced understanding of how key demographic groups distribute themselves among the market's principal sectors and segments, we would have been satisfied with the analytical power of what we had produced. Yet as it turns out, the model does more—a lot more. Using the same graphical lexicon to portray differences and similarities, we asked, "Does the interplay of sectors and segments help shape institutional functions, priorities, and constituencies?" And the answer, again, was yes.

Taken as a whole, figure 2.3 shows that the three characteristics of nontraditional students—part-time degree seekers, distance learners, and undergraduates age 30 or older—all move upward, to the right, across the segments, with very low percentages tightly clustered in the Medallion and Name Brand segments in both the Private and Public sectors, and then becoming higher and dispersing toward the Convenience segment.

We began by focusing on the willingness, and even eagerness, of institutions to pursue the enrollment of part-time degree seekers (the solid lines in figure 2.3). Here, as elsewhere, the more pronounced differences were among the segments, rather than between the sectors. On average, Public colleges and universities were slightly more welcoming of part-time degree seekers—and much more welcoming in the Good Opportunity

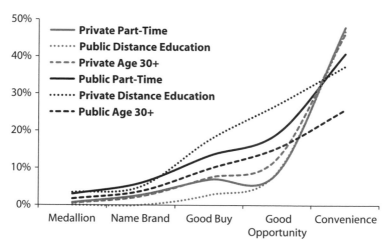

Figure 2.3. Differing forms and populations. *Note*: Public=Four-Year Public; Private=Four-Year Private Not-for-Profit.

segment—than their Private Not-for-Profit counterparts. The important exception—per our definition—occurs in the nation's Convenience institutions. Among Medallion and Name Brand schools, however, whether Public or Private, the proportion of their undergraduate populations who are part-time degree seekers is negligible.

The market segments that enroll large numbers of part-time learners are, for the most part, those with a significant number of institutions enrolling older students. The two sets of curves (the solid and dashed lines in figure 2.3) are nearly parallel and are close together in both the Private and Public sectors. The same strong upward shift is characteristic of the distribution for institutions offering distance education (the dotted lines in figure 2.3). Here, however, there is a sizable gap between the Private and Public sectors in the middle of the market—the Good Buy and Good Opportunity segments. The Public colleges and universities in those segments are more engaged in distance education than their Private counterparts. Overall, what is most striking is the way these three distributions show the extent to which Convenience institutions are distinct from the rest of the market.

We have come to see these upward shifts to the right of the graph as reflecting a major split in the baccalaureate market, each part having its own rationale, demographics, organizational form, and, not at all coincidentally, pricing structure. The right-hand end of the spectrum has the hallmarks of a market of discontinuous shoppers who are willing to enroll at a variety of institutions, often in search of credentials and courses, rather than an integrated path to a degree—what we are calling an emerging spot market for postsecondary education.

Content

Given this interplay of sector and segment attributes, no one should be surprised that what colleges and universities teach can be similarly predicted, once their market sectors and market segments are known. One of the most consistent themes policy advocates echo for changing how American higher education serves the nation is the call for more graduates who have majored in one of the STEM disciplines: science, technology, engineering, and mathematics. What, then, is the distribution across the segments and between the sectors of undergraduates majoring in a STEM discipline? The answer is that segment is more important than

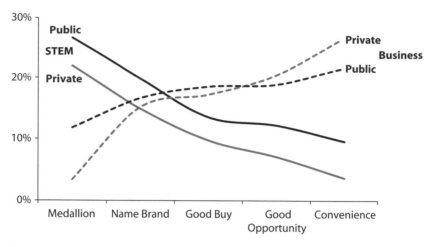

Figure 2.4. STEM and business majors. *Note*: Public=Four-Year Public; Private=Four-Year Private Not-for-Profit.

sector, though Public institutions in comparable segments are slightly more likely to graduate students who had majored in a STEM discipline (the solid lines in figure 2.4).

The other change policy makers are likely to advocate is more emphasis on job skills. To test the degree to which segment and sector played a differentiating role in organizing higher education's more vocational attributes, we graphed the median proportion of business majors for each sector (the dashed lines in figure 2.4) and elicited a near–mirror image of our graph depicting the distribution of STEM majors. Our analysis found that among Private colleges and universities, in particular, one-fourth of the institutions reported that upward of 20 percent of their graduates majored in business, which suggests that those schools were already offering more explicitly vocational majors. On the other hand, a quarter of the Medallion institutions reported no business majors at all.

The Four-Year Private For-Profit Sector

Because the bachelor's degree–granting For-Profit sector (officially named the Four-Year Private For-Profit sector) lacks as clearly defined a structure of segments in which these institutions compete principally with other colleges and universities in the same segment, a sector/segment analysis here does not yield the same kind of predictive results as a similar

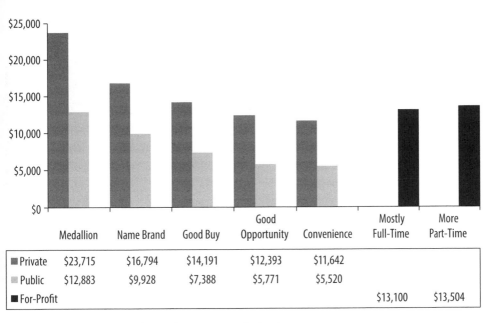

Figure 2.5. Median baccalaureate market prices

analysis of the Public and Private Not-for-Profit sectors. For the Four-Year Private For-Profit sector, we were only able to define two broad segments—institutions characterized by greater part-time enrollments and those more likely to enroll full-time baccalaureate degree seekers. Still, comparisons are both possible and revealing, particularly when they include the average experiences of the two traditional (and larger) baccalaureate sectors. Figure 2.5 displays mean market prices—that is, the average amount of cash per undergraduate student an institution receives—for all segments and sectors of baccalaureate-awarding colleges and universities. For-Profit institutions have priced themselves roughly at the same level as their Private Not-for-Profit Good Buy and Good Opportunity counterparts do, and, not surprisingly, at a noticeably higher level than their Public counterparts.

The more important finding is the extent to which For-Profit institutions now rely on their students' Pell Grants to fund their outreach to prospective enrollees (figure 2.6). The difference between the two market segments in the For-Profit sector is considerably smaller than differences between that sector and other Four-Year sectors. Unlike their Public and

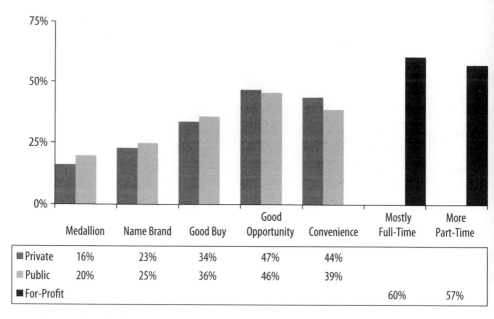

Figure 2.6. Median percentages receiving Pell Grants

Private Not-for-Profit counterparts—even in the Good Opportunity and Convenience segments—the norm in the For-Profit sector is for the majority of full-time enrolled students to have incomes sufficiently low to qualify for Pell Grants.

The For-Profit institutions have similarly strong demographic and ethnic signatures (figure 2.7). At more than half of the For-Profits, African American students made up roughly a quarter of all enrollments—slightly less in the Mostly Full-Time segment, and slightly more in the More Part-Time segment. Hispanic students constituted a much lower percentage of enrolled students in both segments. The enrollment of Asians was negligible.

The For-Profit sector is also characterized by a greater dependence on part-time instructors; a strong appeal to older students; and the vocational nature of the chosen majors, particularly business. While the two segments are similar, the More Part-Time one enrolls a larger percentage of students age 30 or older and business majors and employs more part-time faculty than its corresponding Mostly Full-Time segment.

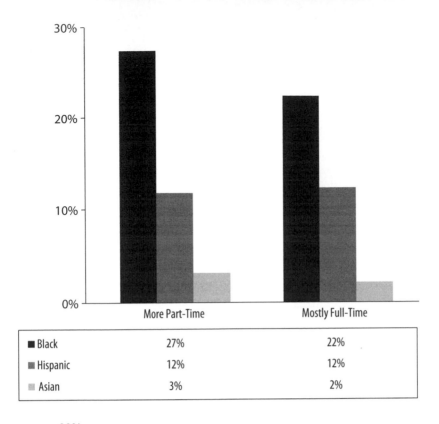

	More Part-Time	Mostly Full-Time
■ Black	27%	22%
■ Hispanic	12%	12%
■ Asian	3%	2%

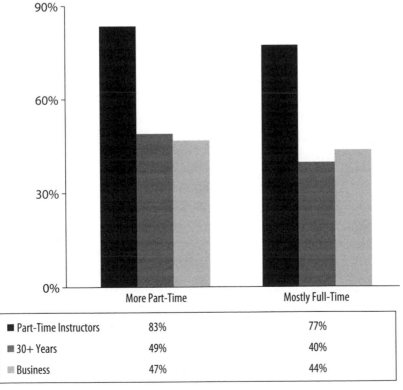

	More Part-Time	Mostly Full-Time
■ Part-Time Instructors	83%	77%
■ 30+ Years	49%	40%
■ Business	47%	44%

Figure 2.7. Four-year Private For-Profit sector ethnicity (*top*) and other characteristics (*bottom*)

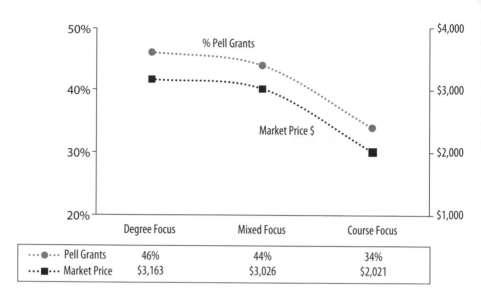

Figure 2.8. Two-Year Public sector median market prices and median percentages of Pell Grant recipients

The Two-Year Public Sector

While the unexplained variance in average market prices predicted by the market segment model was greatest for the Two-Year Public sector, graphing the differences among these institutions yields a noteworthy set of insights. Market prices and the percentage of Pell Grants move in tandem across the sector (left to right) from institutions we defined as Degree Focus to those we labeled Course Focus, reflecting their different pricing strategies and students' varying financial needs (figure 2.8).

In the top quarter of Degree Focus and Mixed Focus institutions, a majority of all full-time students were Pell Grant recipients. In addition, in three-quarters of *all* Two-Year institutions for which we have complete IPEDS data, Pell recipients made up at least a quarter of the total number of students. In one important way, the distribution of Pell recipients across the community college sector differs from their distribution across the baccalaureate market. Whereas the percentage of Pell awardees is smaller in the more traditional segments of the baccalaureate market (figure 2.6), higher proportions of Pell recipients characterize the more traditional Degree Focus two-year colleges.

In figure 2.9, although the ethnic signatures across the Two-Year Public sector differ from those of the baccalaureate market (figure 2.2), three of the other key attributes we have been tracking—proportion of students age 30 years and older, part-time instructors, and part-time degree seekers—behave as they did in the Four-Year sectors (figure 2.3). Hispanic students dominate the Course Focus market, with much of their postsecondary enrollments located in that segment. Black enrollments are more evenly distributed—and, just as in the For-Profit sector (figure 2.7), enrollments by Asians are noticeably low across the sector. Nonresident Alien students are almost totally absent in this sector.

Once again, moving from the Degree Focus to the Course Focus segments yields an increase in nontraditional students—older ones and part-time enrollees—though it is important to note that part-time enrollments were one of the variables we used to differentiate clusters within the Two-Year Public sector. In addition, the Mixed Focus and Course Focus schools rely heavily on part-time faculty, much as was the case in the For-Profits' More Part-Time segment (figure 2.7).

Summing Up

This graphical lexicon provides sufficient detail to allow both institutional leaders and public officials to develop and then employ a more nuanced understanding of the structure of the higher education market in the United States. This understanding, in turn, could guide their efforts to reform undergraduate education now and in the future. Our basic finding is that everything is quite literally (and graphically) connected to everything else. The market forces that began to shape higher education several decades ago have been reinforced over time. The result is a market that is crystalline in its structure and, hence, limiting in terms of the opportunities it offers for changing what colleges and universities are all about.

In thinking of ways in which to guide change across this landscape, we offer two basic axioms. First and foremost, for this market and this enterprise, *one size simply can't fit all*. It is not that institutions are so unique—there is a remarkable commonality among colleges and universities within segments—but it is the segments themselves that are so different. Policies and initiatives that might work to shape the experiences of students choosing to attend a Public or Private Medallion institution could have very different results for different sectors. Moreover, they could quite

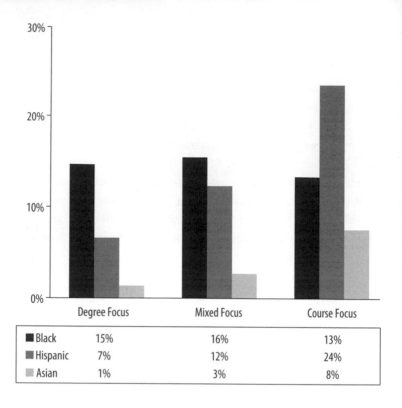

	Degree Focus	Mixed Focus	Course Focus
■ Black	15%	16%	13%
■ Hispanic	7%	12%	24%
■ Asian	1%	3%	8%

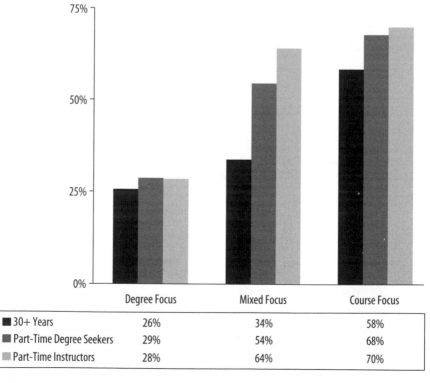

	Degree Focus	Mixed Focus	Course Focus
■ 30+ Years	26%	34%	58%
■ Part-Time Degree Seekers	29%	54%	68%
■ Part-Time Instructors	28%	64%	70%

Figure 2.9. Two-Year Public sector ethnicity (*top*) and populations and part-time faculty (*bottom*)

possibly have negative impacts on the Good Buy and Good Opportunity schools that enroll different kinds of students, often do not teach them the same subjects, and employ faculty in frequently quite dissimilar ways. For example, financial incentives that reward institutions for increasing the numbers of STEM majors would favor the Medallion and Name Brand segments (both Public and Private), because they already have the faculty and a curriculum in place to teach this material.

Second, *change will require altering not just one or two attributes, but simultaneously reshaping almost every key attribute that matters.* The hard edges of the market represent formidable barriers that are themselves the product of patterns and predilections deeply engrained within the nature of nearly every institution. To focus on the most obvious for a moment, consider again the intertwining of completion rates, market prices, and ethnicity. These are attributes that, on the one hand, co-vary with each other while, at the same time, are highly predictive of institutional curricula, faculty organization, technological adaptation, and the attraction of enrolling older and part-time learners. Shifts in one attribute will inevitably result in transformations to nearly every other attribute, whether intended or not. In other words, it is hard to imagine an initiative that would change the curriculum of an institution but leave its demographic profile in place.

The larger lesson, then, is woe to the would-be reformer who does not understand the workings of the market for undergraduate education across the nation. And that, plainly put, is the market imperative all aspiring reformers face.

3

Student Consumers

The small article by Beckie Supiano (2014) was almost lost among the torrent of comment stirred up by a White House determined to make colleges and universities more responsive to consumer demands. What distinguished this piece was its quiet skepticism, a willingness to ask unanswered questions, and a fundamental doubt about whether the market for undergraduate education in the United States requires more consumer information. Supiano began by noting that there had already been a "proliferation of consumer information," most of which takes "for granted that prospects will embark on a broad, national search" for just the right college or university, much like they might shop around "for a car or some other big-ticket consumer item." And then she hit her target, observing that for many students, their choice of a college is not among thousands of institutions nationwide, nor those schools at the top of *US News & World Report*'s rankings. Instead, "it's the contained, sometimes even sparse, group of colleges within a reasonable radius of home" (Supiano 2014). We might have added that this search is confined to a single—or perhaps two adjacent—market segments, often consisting of remarkably similar institutions.

At one time, we believed that the consumer—and probably the consumer alone—could provide an effective counterbalance to the market forces that were beginning to bear down on an enterprise composed, for the most part, of institutions unprepared for the rigors of market competition. What higher education needed was smarter shoppers, as well as something of its own, resembling *Consumer Reports*, that would allow shoppers to compare the educational products of the nation's colleges and universities.

It was not that collegiate shoppers lacked detailed information about the thousands of institutions to which they might apply. The problem was not volume, but format. Most of the information came in thick tomes, with small print that resembled the *Oxford Unabridged Dictionary*: books such as *Barron's*, *Peterson's*, and the College Board's *College Handbook*. The 2016 version of the *Handbook* claims near-encyclopedic completeness by observing that it is the only guide that "contains objective information on every accredited college in the United States—2,200 four-year colleges and universities, and 1,700 two-year community colleges and technical schools." Containing over 40 indices, the *Handbook* boasts that it is "the fastest, easiest way for students to narrow a college search and compare the schools that they're interested in" (Amazon.com presentation of *College Handbook* 2016).

Thirty years ago, the first to break this pattern was Edward Fiske, the education editor for the *New York Times*. Fiske saw the emergence of an increasingly competitive market for the nation's best students and their often financially well-off parents or grandparents. What his *Fiske Guide to Colleges* continues to promote is "an insider's look at the academic climates, student body demographics, dorms and social life, and for all the top schools—including the strengths and weaknesses (something you won't see on college websites) and Fiske's exclusive quality-of-life ratings" (Amazon.com presentation of the *Fiske Guide to Colleges 2014*). Today, the Fiske guides have become a publishing franchise, offering, among other titles, a *Fiske Countdown to College: 41 To-Do Lists and a Plan for Every Year of High School*, a *Fiske Guide to Getting into the Right College*, *Fiske Real College Essays that Work*, a *Fiske Guide to Colleges with Great Sports Traditions*, and a *Fiske Guide to Colleges: 2014 Best Buys*.

Fiske clearly aimed his guides at students interested in top colleges, regardless of price. His enterprise focused on the 300 most competitive colleges in the United States. The majority of institutions in that select company were seldom shy about touting a Fiske observation in their recruitment materials. Because the guides were entertainingly written, they quickly found a market that has proven to be more enduring than the mega-volumes of the 1970s and 1980s.

Enter the Rankings

The really big seller, however, has been the annual rankings—as opposed to ratings—supplied by *US News & World Report*. Though their origin is now largely forgotten, the *US News* rankings began life as a sophisticated "smile" survey, which asked college and university presidents to rank institutions with which their schools competed. From the outset, the rankings were about being the *best* in one of two categories: universities, and colleges. Not reticent about making fine-grade distinctions, *US News* claimed that it objectively evaluated colleges and universities in terms of their quality.

The astonishing result was that *US News* became *the* arbiter of the college-choice process—for students and their families, and for institutions striving to maintain their position in an increasingly competitive market for students in general and, in particular, for those who could pay the full or near-full price for a college education. When we developed our first market segment models in the late 1990s, we pondered how well our segmentation matched up with the *US News* rankings of the nation's "best colleges." By knowing an institution's five-year graduation rate and, hence, its market segment, would you also know how it placed in the *US News* rankings? By knowing an institution's ranking, would you know its market segment and, hence, the price it was able to charge? The answer in both cases was yes, suggesting that the "rankings game" measures market position and little else (*Change* 2003).

Analyzing the top 25 liberal arts colleges and the top 25 universities separately, we constructed our own ranking, using only the graduation rates. We then compared the two rankings: the one presented by *US News* for each group, and the other, composed of a "predicted rank" that we constructed. The results were quite dramatic. Among the top liberal arts colleges, more than one-third either retained exactly the same ranking or appeared no more than one slot below or above. Nearly half of the institutions had predicted ranks that fell less than two spots away from the one in *US News*, and 21 of the 25 fell fewer than four rungs below their *US News* ranking. For the top 25 universities, the findings were not quite as arresting. For two-thirds of the top 25 universities, the difference between their *US News* rank and our predicted one was three places or less. We then concluded that what matters in the rankings are the applicants who partition the market. Institutions, contrary to their stated goals of diversity, turn out to be far more homogenous in terms of their students' ambitions, expectations, and preparation. We concluded that "if an institution wants to change its rankings, it could follow two general strategies: increase its visibility and reputation, or improve retention through better programs or the judicious use of merit scholarships to attract more competitive students" (*Change* 2003, 58).

Attempts to Measure Quality

No doubt unintentionally, *US News* also provoked a renewed interest in actually testing the quality of American higher education. The way to fight "rankings mania" and, not incidentally, help colleges and universities improve their educational product was to develop real measures of institutional quality, rather than the surrogates for prestige and status that lay at the core of the *US News* rankings. The first decade of this century saw three major attempts to gauge quality. Russell Edgerton and Peter Ewell's National Survey of Student Engagement (NSSE) asked a large sample of students to assess their educational experiences. Our own College Results Survey (CRS) invited the alumni of a select set of institutions to evaluate their confidence in their ability to complete tasks for which college was supposed to have prepared them. The Council for Aid to Education introduced the Collegiate Learning Assessment (CLA), an attempt to do what the NSSE and the CRS deliberately eschewed—gauge educational effectiveness by actually testing both beginning and graduating students, to document just how much learning takes place between initial enrollment and graduation. Versions of both the NSSE and the CLA continue to be employed today, despite some serious obstacles and criticism. The CRS did not survive the decade.

The National Survey of Student Engagement, first unveiled in 2000 under the joint sponsorship of the Pew Charitable Trusts and the Carnegie Foundation for the Advancement of Teaching, was the inspiration of Russell Edgerton, chief educational officer for the Pew Charitable Trusts, and Peter Ewell of the National Center for Higher Education Management Systems (NCHEMS), who, by the 1990s, had become the leading advocate for an evidence-based focus on learning outcomes. Edgerton and Ewell argued that a decade of solid research had identified the kinds of practices that promoted student learning. Discovering which institutions were employing those practices would produce a list of the ones with strong learning outcomes. This initial survey was administered to more than 63,000 seniors at a wide variety of colleges and universities across the country. Respondents were asked to report their experiences in terms of five clusters, each representing a different national benchmark for effective educational practice: (1) the level of academic challenge, (2) the amount of active and collaborative learning, (3) student interactions with faculty members, (4) the degree of access to enriching educational experiences, and (5) the level of campus support.

From the outset, the NSSE faced a host of challenges, including the reluctance of colleges and universities to participate if the results were to be made public. To provide a tangible sense of how and what the NSSE was measuring, the survey's organizers instead identified those institutions with the best results in each of the survey's benchmarked categories. And that decision quickly revealed a second problem. The four schools featured in the NSSE's initial report—Beloit College, Centre College, Elon University, and Sweet Briar College—were hardly household names; none, for example, were top rated, or even highly ranked, in *US News & World Report*. Making the most of this situation, the NSSE's first director, George Kuh, said: "There are some really hidden jewels out there. . . . One surprise was that some high-profile schools don't do as well as some schools that most people have never heard of" (Reisberg 2000). Throughout its history, the NSSE would struggle in trying to persuade the industry's leaders to participate and share their results publicly.

Instead, the NSSE has become something of a champion of small liberal arts colleges, which were found to be "more demanding academically, requiring more writing and more analytical thinking than other types of colleges" (Reisberg 2000). In contrast to liberal arts colleges, large universities were less apt to be successful in engaging students in collaborative learning. Still, the NSSE's creators stressed that the immediate goal of the survey was to help colleges and universities identify their strengths and weaknesses, as their students perceive them.

At about the same time, we introduced the College Results Survey, jointly sponsored by the National Center for Postsecondary Improvement and the Knight Higher Education Collaborative. The CRS resembled the NSSE in that it was a survey administered to a sample of 1991–92 graduates of 80 colleges and universities who participated in the programs of the Knight Higher Education Collaborative. Unlike the NSSE, however, the CRS sample was disproportionately filled with individuals from the nation's Medallion colleges and universities, though in terms of the occupations of its respondents—now six or more years beyond their bachelor's degree—the CRS group closely paralleled the distribution of occupations for all college graduates 27 to 30 years old, as reported by the US Bureau of Labor Statistics.

Unlike the NSSE, the CRS more directly asked its respondents to judge how their college educations shaped their lives after graduation. In the broadest sense, the question posed to these alumni was simple: "How confident do you feel about doing the things a college education is supposed to prepare you to do?" Our findings can be summarized as follows:

- Roughly two out of three college graduates (63 percent) felt confident in their ability to organize information and communicate its meaning to others.
- Nearly as many (61 percent) felt confident in their ability to perform quantitative tasks and analyses.
- But less than half (48 percent) felt confident in their ability to find information—in essence, the skills needed to research a topic.

The CRS taught three invaluable lessons, but only one was what we hoped to learn. First, it was possible in a survey to develop a rough gauge of the effectiveness of an individual institution. We were quite familiar with most of the colleges and universities that participated in the CRS experiment—and we knew in advance the kind of answers we expected from their graduates. The poster child for this part of our experiment was Hamilton College in upstate New York, an institution that had made written and oral presentations a hallmark of its curriculum. And sure enough, Hamilton graduates outscored those of all the other participating institutions on the section that measured writing/presenting work skills.

The second lesson was that the CRS results were less helpful to the sponsoring institutions than we had hoped. The problem was essentially one of timeliness. We had responded to the market by developing an instrument that gathered information from alumni just after they had their job and learning skills tested in the labor market. But we were also evaluating curricula that were 5 to 10 years old—more than enough time to have the institutions say, "We have already changed our curricula," whether they had actually done so or not. "Nice try," we were told, but, in the end, not all that helpful.

Third, we learned that there really wasn't a market for what we had so painstakingly produced. The public roll-out of the CRS results started with a bang—a two-page–plus article and picture in *Time* magazine—which resulted in a visit from Michael Brannick, who was then the CEO of Peterson's Publishing. In relatively quick order, Peterson's licensed the CRS, with intentions of soliciting colleges and universities to participate and making the results an integral part of future issues of *Peterson's Guide*. This never worked, despite substantial investments on both our part and the technology staff at Peterson's. Once Peterson's abandoned the project, we recruited a small set of follow-up institutions, in order to test whether a web-administered survey of alumni would have an acceptable response rate. The answer, alas, was no—by then most people had become sufficiently suspicious of web products that requested detailed individual data. Whereas the original CRS, a pencil and paper survey, had enjoyed a 30 to 60 percent response rate (in general, Public institution response rates were lower than those from Private ones), our web-administered survey, which had come with the same imprimatur of the sponsoring institutions, suffered from response rates of 10 percent or less. And so the CRS died.

The third, well-funded national initiative to develop a reasonable means of measuring the educational effectiveness of the nation's colleges and universities was launched at nearly the same time as the NSSE and the CRS. The Collegiate Learning Assessment is a complex, computer-based test that requires a skilled cadre of scorers to produce its estimate of student learning. As described by the National Institute for Learning Outcomes Assessment, the CLA is a test of reasoning and communication skills at the institutional level, to determine how a college or university as a whole contributes to student development. It focuses on the value-added aspect of attending that institution by evaluating performance and analytical writing tasks, with the latter covering critical thinking, reasoning, written communication, and problem solving (NILOA 2015).

The CLA, which most observers believed primarily measured critical thinking, owed much of its initial attention to two disconnected events. The first was a quasi endorsement in 2006 by the Spellings Commission, which saluted the CLA for "using performance tasks and writing prompts rather than multiple choice questions" to gauge "students' critical thinking, analytic reasoning, and written communication." In the eyes of the authors of the commission's final report, a salient factor was that the CLA measured "value added between the freshman and senior years." Just as importantly, the CLA's unit of analysis was "the institution and not the student," and its results allowed "inter-institutional comparisons that show how each institution contributes to learning" (US Department of Education 2006, 23).

The second event was the publication of Richard Arum and Josipa Roksa's *Academically Adrift* (2011a), which had used results from the administration of the Collegiate Learning Assessment to 2,300 college freshmen and sophomores at two dozen four-year colleges and universities. The lesson *Academically Adrift* taught was probably best summed up by Louis Soares in support of Arum and Roksa's call for disruptive innovations. What *Academically Adrift* demonstrated, according to Soares, was that

- 45 percent of the students they followed "demonstrated no significant gains in critical thinking, analytical reasoning, and written communications during the first two years of college";
- 32 percent did not, in a typical semester, take "any courses with more than 40 pages of reading per week"; and
- 50 percent "did not take a single course in which they wrote more than 20 pages over the course of the semester" (Soares 2011).

Writing in the *New York Times*, Arum and Roksa made clear the link between their analysis and the sentiment of most of higher education's critics: that students didn't learn, which meant that colleges and universities were not adding value. "We found that large numbers of the students were making their way through college with minimal exposure to rigorous coursework, only a modest investment of effort and little or no meaningful improvement in skills like writing and reasoning" (Arum and Roksa 2011b).

Ultimately, the high-stakes claim that the CLA could do what higher education had so long insisted was not possible drew attention to what proved to be the CLA's wobbly methodology. Scholars with a technical interest in assessment were already worried about the high correlation between SAT scores and CLA results. There were open doubts that individual-level data could be mustered in such a way as to yield valid measures of an institution's collective contribution to the learning of all of its students. We, along with others, fussed that it was not possible to view as valid the results of an assessment where the results had no direct consequence to its participants. And that was precisely what the CLA did, because those who took the CLA on behalf of their institutions were repeatedly assured that the findings would not affect their subsequent education or careers.

The more telling blow, however, came from Braden J. Hosch of Central Connecticut State University. Central Connecticut was one of four institutions in that state administering the CLA to a sample of its students as part of the Voluntary System of Accountability project of the Association of Public and Land-Grant Universities and the American Association of State Colleges and Universities. What Hosch noticed when reviewing three years of CLA results for his institution was a remarkably strong correlation between the amount of time a student took to complete the CLA and that student's score. Hosch's observation implied that what the CLA may very well be measuring is not learning, but motivation. In addition, institutions that have administered the CLA have almost uniformly acknowledged that eliciting a representative sample of students to take this test has proven to be a major problem. The answer, the *Chronicle of Higher Education* reported, was to turn to "low-level bribery. Seniors who volunteer to take the test now have their $40 cap-and-gown fees waived" (Glenn 2010). What Hosch had come to suspect was that students who took their bribe and breezed through the test got lower scores than those students who, having been challenged by the CLA, took the test seriously and, as a result, earned higher scores.

The Rankings Persist

In the meantime, *US News & World Report* soldiered on—expanding its ranking empire, fending off the persistent criticisms these rankings received, and growing increasingly secure in the knowledge that it had supplied what the market wanted. Here again it is helpful to ask, "Just what do the *US News* rankings measure that those comprising the market— parents, students, the media, and, to a surprising degree, policy wonks— really want?" To answer that question, we have now replicated our 2003 analysis, comparing the rankings with the results we derived from our market segment/market sector analysis. This time, we had more institutions to include: 203 "national" universities and 178 "national" liberal arts

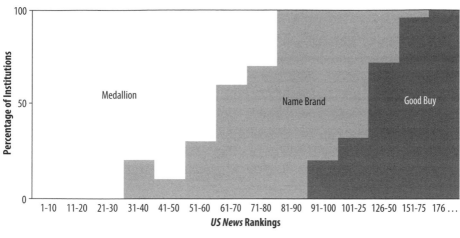

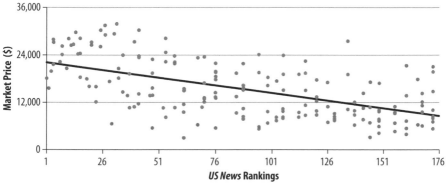

Figure 3.1. National university rankings versus market segments (*top*) and market prices (*bottom*)

colleges. The results of that comparison are basically the same as in our original analysis. In the top display in figure 3.1, we have plotted the market segment of each of the universities to which *US News* assigned a specific ranking. As in so much of the other aspects of our analysis on the impacts of segments and sectors on the shape of US higher education, the result was an almost perfectly ordered set. The 30 top-ranked universities (according to *US News*) were all Medallion institutions. With a single exception, the 101 lowest-ranked colleges and universities were all in our Good Buy segment. Squeezed between the Medallions and the Good Buys were the Name Brands. Given the correlation between an institution's market

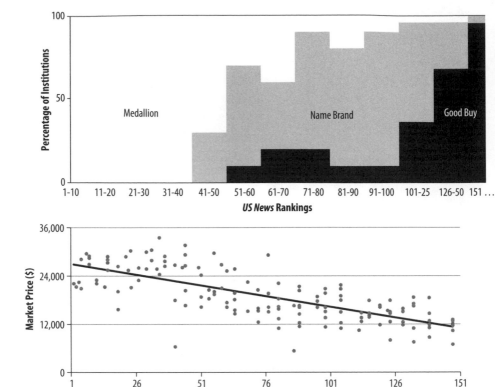

Figure 3.2. National liberal arts college rankings versus market segments (*top*) and market prices (*bottom*)

price and its market segment, no one should be surprised that a *US News* ranking could also be used to guess an institution's market price.

We can extend this analysis by matching institutions in terms of their *US News* rankings and their market prices—that is, the amount of funds an institution receives, on average, for each full-time undergraduate. For the *US News* rankings, the match with the market segment results is tidier for the national liberal arts colleges (figure 3.2), largely because of the near absence of public institutions among liberal arts colleges. (In figures 3.1 and 3.2, the market segment data came from IPEDS' 2012 report and the rankings data from 2014 rankings in *US News*.)

Taken together, figures 3.1 and 3.2 help explain the sustained popularity of the *US News* rankings. Recall the observation made by the *Chronicle of Higher Education* reporter with which we began this chapter: that these rankings, dreaded or not, were really only important for a small portion of the market—those students and their families prepared to "embark on a broad, national search," that is, those would-be consumers who are "shopping around, just as they might for a car or some other big-ticket consumer item, and that . . . [are] willing to pick up and move anywhere in the country" (Supiano 2014). The *US News* rankings give these shoppers all they really want or need: an estimate of an institution's prestige, on the one hand, and, on the other, a pretty good estimate of the market price these schools are likely to charge and how hard it will be to gain admission to a particular college or university. In other words, the higher the ranking of that institution, the higher the price and the lower the probability of admission.

The Diminished Importance of Consumer Information

Though we certainly wish it were otherwise, our conclusion is that a search for consumer information that would help students and their families become better higher education shoppers, while also helping institutions plan how to improve their products, has proven to be a chimera. The idea that smart shoppers would compel higher education to be more responsive to student learning, as well as ultimately restrain increases in the prices colleges and universities charged their undergraduates, has simply not materialized—nor is it likely to do so in the future.

Does that mean that our market segment model only has a limited utility? No, but the model does have a *different* utility. What it describes, in remarkably precise terms, are the contours of the market for undergraduate education in the United States. As we pointed out in the conclusion of chapter 2, the undergraduate student market has a crystalline structure. The result is that the leaders of the nation's colleges and universities, along with the public officials responsible for an increasingly national system of higher education, confront a market that repeatedly limits their opportunities to change what America's postsecondary institutions are all about.

The constituency most in need of absorbing these lessons is the federal government and its Department of Education, which has a long history of not being able to shoot straight. Nearly thirty years ago, *Policy Perspectives*, a publication of the Pew Higher Education Roundtable, argued that there are just three fundamental issues that ought to concern those who seek the continuous improvement of the nation's colleges and universities: (1) costs, (2) teaching and learning, and (3) what the Pew Roundtable identified as "sorting" and now goes by the more understandable label of access. *Policy Perspectives* summed up the importance of these issues for the nation at large by observing that the first priority, controlling costs, is at odds with the other two goals, which are improving teaching and learning, and expanding access. Institutions that manage their resources better, and increase their productivity through the use of technology and other means, will want to plow the savings into an enhanced quality for their scholarly priorities, rather than their social or instructional goals. It noted, however, that "if scholarship is to make advances in areas vital to the interests of all parts of society, then all parts of society need to participate in higher education," recommending that "the broad issues of educational quality and social equity be considered in tandem and recognized as truly interdependent" (PHERP 1988).

What the Pew Roundtable asked for is neither more nor less than what most policy makers seek today. The tough, truly divisive issue concerns the means to achieve those ends. What lingers in the minds of many, both in Washington, DC, and across the community of policy advocates, is the elusive hope that shoppers who become smarter through the ready availability of useful consumer information will make the nation's colleges and universities alter their behavior.

What we see, instead, is that changes to higher education will require additional regulation and a much more targeted—and probably costlier—program of federal aid. And it will require the government's willingness to intervene directly in the functioning of the postsecondary education market. What will not help are better net price calculators or improved (or even just different) rankings or ratings of institutions, unless these measurements provide direct and meaningful financial rewards to the institutions being ranked and rated.

4

Jobs

The new gold standard for a college education is the assurance upon graduation of not just a job, but a well-paying job, one capable of generating sufficient income to allow a recent graduate to pay off the loans that helped underwrite the cost of his or her baccalaureate degree. What students and their parents—especially their parents—want to know is what kinds of jobs a new college graduate can expect on entering the labor market.

Thus it was hardly surprising when the Brookings Institution announced what it was sure would prove to be an impressive double: a new college-ranking system that challenged *US News & World Report*'s hegemony while simultaneously providing detailed information on the labor market experiences of recent graduates of more than 3,000 American postsecondary institutions. Brookings' *Beyond College Rankings: A Value-Added Approach to Assessing Two- and Four-Year Schools* promised a permanent shift in how the public came to view college quality. Henceforth, the economic advantage a college or university conferred on its graduates would replace prestige as the principal metric determining that institution's standing. As an additional bonus, the Brookings ranking marked a wholesale embrace of new social media tools as a means of generating the kind of economic-tracking data that policy makers had long sought. For Jonathan Rothwell and Siddharth Kulkarni, the creators of Brookings' *Value-Added Rankings*, the importance of their work lay in its confirmation that it was possible to test the promises colleges and universities were making for both the long- and short-term values of their degrees. The authors' premise was that a college's "polices and programs" have effects not only on students' lives, but also on the community in which that school is located. They claimed that student support, both financial and otherwise, "can dramatically boost graduation rates and thus future student success" (Rothwell and Kulkarni 2015, 2). In addition, they argued that a college's curriculum and its major offerings are strong predictors of students' ultimate earnings. By gathering data about these characteristics—curriculum and support—they could help institutions understand and improve student outcomes. What enabled their project to succeed, the authors argued, was their willingness to consider data sources hitherto excluded from the tool kits of those exploring the economic impact of a college education.

For economic, skills, and collegiate data, they turned to such websites as PayScale and LinkedIn. They added information from College Measures, a service that provided an array of information, including income data for recent alumni in six states. Acknowledging that these sources were imperfect, Rothwell and Kulkarni nonetheless understood that they offered a way to add an important dimension to traditional college assessments. For these Brookings researchers, LinkedIn and PayScale became the social media of choice, with the latter providing the most robust data: "PayScale appears to be the most promising. In exchange for a free 'salary report'—showing how a user's earnings stack up against peers in his or her field—anyone can create an account on PayScale after entering information on where they attended school, what they studied, and how much they earn" (Rothwell and Kulkarni 2015, 3).

Less than a week later, Anthony Carnevale, Ban Cheah, and Andrew Hanson of the Georgetown University Center on Education and the Workforce published *The Economic Value of College Majors* (2015), their own answer to what had become the industry's dominant question, "What is a college education worth?" Carnevale and his colleagues' answer was straightforward—almost deceptively simple. Graduates who had majored in certain fields received higher initial salaries that almost always translated into higher lifetime earnings. Engineering and architecture majors, when employed full time, were the best paid. Education majors were paid the least. Employed business majors varied the most in terms of their compensation. Nearly four out of five college graduates majored in what Carnevale and his colleagues labeled a "career-focused field." And while the proportion of students majoring in the humanities and the liberal arts had declined, the number of students taking courses in these fields had gone up, "due to more rigorous general education requirements." The Georgetown Center's researchers claimed that "deciding what to major in is more important than deciding whether to attend college" (Carnevale, Cheah, and Hanson 2015, 4). They explained that while there was a $1 million difference in average earnings between high school and college graduates, the differences across college majors was even larger. For example, those with a petroleum engineering degree could expect to earn almost three and a half times the $1.4 million earned by someone with an early childhood education degree.

While intrigued by this analysis, our own reading of the data, much of which was also used by the Brookings and Georgetown projects, lead us to conclude that the Georgetown study was surprisingly incomplete and the Brookings rankings wondrously wrongheaded. For all of its inventiveness and intriguing use of social media data, Brookings' *Value-Added Rankings* fall victim to two fundamental problems. First, as a number of commentators were quick to point out, it was not at all clear that the authors actually had access to reliable data reporting both the starting and continuing salaries of the graduates of the nation's two- and four-year postsecondary institutions. Both PayScale and LinkedIn provide incomplete and self-biased information detailing the current occupations and salaries of those who voluntarily report their personal information to these sites. In general, assembling individual-specific salary records that can then be matched with collegiate enrollment and graduate data has proven to be an analytically as well as a politically messy task. In some states there have been attempts to correlate college degree information with employment/unemployment data that include personal incomes, but those have floundered, sometimes because the data were state specific or because of the near impossibility of identifying the institution—and often the multiple institutions—each person in the employment/unemployment records attended, and sometimes because the record system had fallen victim to a state's need to reduce the cost of its government. To their credit, Rothwell and Kulkarni tried to verify the data drawn from the social media sites by comparing the distributions of majors, occupations, and salaries with those published by the US Bureau of Labor Statistics (BLS). What could not be similarly verified was matching of those distributions with the alumni of specific colleges, universities, and technical schools.

The second problem with this approach derives from our own findings, where it is not the individual college or university granting the degree or the specific major completed at a given institution that makes the difference, but rather the particular domain—either sector or segment—a student enrolls in and graduates from that matters most. As we have sought to make clear in our discussion of how the segments and sectors slice and dice the American market for an undergraduate education, the predictive and (in that particular sense) really important differences are those that separate segments and sectors, rather than those that distinguish between or among individual institutions and programs. College and university profiles within the same market segment are nearly always similar, often verging on being almost identical. Perhaps the easiest way to demonstrate that similarity is to again focus on the rate at which Four-Year institutions in the Public and Private Not-for-Profit sectors graduate STEM (science, technical, engineering, and mathematics) majors, on the one hand, and business majors, on the other.

We have already illustrated just how dramatically different the educational experiences at Medallion and Name Brand institutions can be from those at Good Buy, Good Opportunity, and Convenience ones (chapter 2). Among Four-Year Private Not-for-Profit colleges and universities, the proportion of STEM majors drops steadily and precipitously from a median of nearly one-quarter among Medallion institutions to a negligible 4 percent among Convenience ones. The left-to-right decline is equally sharp for Four-Year Public institutions. In contrast, the curves for business majors reverse the pattern, ascending from left to right. This rise is most dramatic when Private Not-for-Profit institutions are included, indicating that for this attribute, sector was almost as important as segment. The lesson for policy makers and reformers is equally clear. Policies and initiatives focusing on STEM fields will probably confer the greatest advantage to Medallion and Name Brand institutions in both sectors. Initiatives and policies that focus on business majors will most likely benefit Good Buy, Good Opportunity, and Convenience colleges and universities in both sectors.

Our focus on segment and sector also frames our differences with the Georgetown University study, which linked college majors and postgraduation incomes. In many ways our work and that of the university's Center on Education and the Workforce parallel one another, in that each focuses on majors and utilizes reporting by the BLS on the average earnings of college graduates within specific majors. To disaggregate the BLS data by sectors and segments, however, requires a more complex methodology than that employed by the Georgetown team. But the payoff is a much clearer portrait of the job market landscape for college graduates.

The analysis that follows draws on data available from two governmental agencies. The National Center for Education Statistics (NCES), through IPEDS, provides an extensive array of completion data, detailing the distribution of collegiate degrees by fields of study (majors). The Bureau of Labor Statistics supplies detailed data on occupations, employment, and wages. A mapping, or crosswalk, between IPEDS completions (Classification of Instructional Programs, or CIP), and BLS occupations (Standard Occupational Classification, or SOC), is available on the IPEDS Data Center website (NCES 2010). Armed with that information and knowing the distribution of graduates by sector, segment, and major (a two-digit CIP) we were able to answer the question, given the distribution of majors across different segments and sectors, is it likely that these students will face differing employment prospects?

We started with basic information, tracking the economic value of specific collegiate majors in terms of the median salaries of recent graduates with limited or no labor market experience (table 4.1). As noted in the Georgetown study, the best-paid majors are in engineering and engineering-related fields, followed by computer and information sciences. The classic liberal arts majors—which include history and English language and literature—are clumped somewhere in the middle. The majors that once were thought to frame a commitment to doing good—education; theology and religious vocations; and parks, recreation, leisure, and fitness studies— were clustered near the bottom of the list. The full set is an intriguing reflection of just how varied and different the jobs of recent college graduates can be. No doubt the most obvious is the gap between the best-paid majors (roughly $130,000 for the top engineering fields) and the least paid (around $28,000 for those focusing on parks, recreation, leisure, and fitness activities). Yet there can be a substantial variance even within a broad field, depending on the particular specialty. For example, in 2012, the median salary for petroleum engineers was $130,280, while cost estimators— a job for which an engineering major may be a requisite—had a median

Table 4.1. Median annual wages (2012) by undergraduate major for recent college graduates with no prior experience

	Median in lowest paying field ($)	Median in highest paying field ($)
Top five, based on weighted average of median wages		
Engineering	58,860	130,280
Engineering technologies and engineering-related fields	57,440	99,000
Computer and information sciences and support services	44,150	99,000
Health professions and related programs	39,980	92,030
Biological and biomedical sciences	44,770	90,060
Selected others, based on weighted average of median wages		
Business management, marketing, and related support services	39,420	93,680
Homeland security, law enforcement, other protective services	41,530	81,140
English language and literature/letters	55,050	55,940
History	38,220	55,050
Education	28,360	76,540
Bottom five, based on weighted average of median wages		
Agriculture, agriculture operations and related sciences	35,870	66,260
Area, ethnic, cultural, gender, and group studies	45,430	45,430*
Theology and religious vocations	26,380	44,060
Science technologies/technicians	39,750	39,750*
Parks, recreation, leisure, and fitness studies	28,360	44,770

Note: Graduates selected from 29 majors and sorted high to low, using the weighted average of the median in the subfields.
*Categories with only one subfield reported.

salary of $58,860. Civil engineering, the field in which the largest number of engineers are employed, carried a median salary of $100,920. By contrast, the vast majority of jobs held by those with parks, recreation, leisure, and fitness studies majors carried a median salary of $28,360. Less than 10 percent of those jobs were in the occupations of athletic trainer or exercise physiologist, which provided median salaries in the low $40,000s. Nonetheless, the lowest paid jobs held by engineering majors had substan-

Table 4.2. Ten largest majors in the analysis (%)

	Medallion	Name Brand	Good Buy	Good Opportunity	Convenience
Four-Year Public					
Business	12	17	19	19	25
Social sciences	15	10	8	6	6
Health professions	4	5	8	11	11
Visual and performing arts	4	4	5	4	2
Psychology	7	7	6	6	7
Education	2	5	8	9	6
Biological/biomedical sciences	10	7	5	5	4
Communications	5	6	5	4	3
Engineering	9	8	4	2	2
English	4	4	3	3	3
Four-Year Private Not-for-Profit					
Business	13	19	19	25	34
Social sciences	17	10	5	4	2
Health professions	4	9	12	12	14
Visual and performing arts	7	7	10	6	1
Psychology	6	7	6	7	8
Education	1	5	7	9	5
Biological/biomedical sciences	9	7	5	4	2
Communications	5	7	5	3	2
Engineering	8	4	3	0	1
English	4	4	3	2	1

tially higher median salaries than the highest paid ones for parks, recreation, leisure, and fitness studies majors.

The list of majors we worked with was necessarily abbreviated, including only those for which the Bureau of Labor Statistics provided adequate data to perform its analysis. Even so, our overall list is longer than it needs to be, since just 10 majors account for nearly three-quarters of the graduates from both Private Not-for-Profit and Public baccalaureate institutions—albeit in slightly different proportions in each sector (table 4.2). Across the Private For-Profit schools, the range of majors is even more limited—in all, just five majors account for more than three-quarters of all of their baccalaureate graduates.

Here again, there are important differences among the segments, rather than between the sectors. Moving from the Medallion to Convenience segments, business becomes the increasingly dominant major, on average accounting for one out of every three or four bachelor's degrees from Private or Public Convenience institutions. The numbers of social and biological sciences majors drop off considerably. While engineering is not a top five major in any segment, it nearly disappears entirely among the Good Buy, Good Opportunity, and Convenience segments. Similarly, education barely registers in the Medallion segment, but it becomes an increasingly important major across the various segments, peaking in the Good Opportunity institutions.

The distribution of principal majors across the Private For-Profit sector closely resembles the distribution within the Convenience and Good Opportunity segments in the Public and Private Not-for-Profit baccalaureate sectors, only more so. Business majors account for 40 percent of the For-Profit sector's baccalaureate degree production. Health professions are a distant second, with just 13 percent of the graduates. Note that homeland security, law enforcement, firefighting, and related protective services appear in the For-Profit list but not in the tables reflecting the most preferred majors in the Four-Year Public and Private Not-for-Profit sectors.

We next sought to gauge the economic value of each segment's portfolio of majors. The necessary calculation was straightforward enough. For any segment, we computed an average salary by weighting the median salary associated with the occupations related to each major by the number of majors in the segment. On one level, the results were as expected—the average starting salaries (as estimated by the percentage of these majors among all the graduates in each segment) increased, for the most part, monotonically from Convenience through Medallion institutions for both the Public and Private Not-for-Profit sectors. On the other hand, the differences between the average starting salaries in each segment were quite small—perhaps because we had to assign the median salary to everyone, or perhaps because newly minted college graduates entering the labor market believe that a job is a job. What is important at the start of the process is not "What is the starting salary?" but, rather, "Will I like it?" or "Can I do the required work?" Only later does the potential compensation level enter the picture, and then only after the would-be graduate has made most of the decisions that will probably determine his or her future employability.

Does It Really Matter?

All of which raises the question, "Does it really matter?" There is no evidence that either students or parents want or need more or better or more finely tuned consumer data. The same is true for the kind of market/ job data that is so much in vogue today. We doubt that there would be many college-bound students or their parents who would be surprised by the levels of salaries presented in table 4.1. Knowing that engineers make more money is not likely to increase either applications to or graduations from accredited engineering programs. And it certainly is no great revelation that teachers and recreation supervisors are at or near the bottom of the list in terms of starting salaries.

It appears that more or better labor market data is neither likely to spur educational reform nor persuade consumers to make different choices. Yet we were struck by two articles, appearing in the spring of 2015, that proclaimed new insights into the nature of the postcollegiate labor market. The first was a Q and A session conducted by *Inside Higher Ed*'s Jake New with Northwestern University professor of management Lauren Rivera. The subject was Rivera's recently published book, with the evocative title *Pedigree: How Elite Students Get Elite Jobs*. It was not so much Rivera's argument that caught our eye as New's summary of it: "Despite merit-based college admissions, equal opportunity employment regulations and the long-held idea that in America, hard work is the key to social mobility, affluent graduates from elite institutions are still often the ones who find the highest-paying entry-level jobs" (New 2015). He went on to say that Rivera's attempt to understand why includes a "candid look at why top-tier investment banks, consulting firms and law firms make the hiring decisions they do—and how when firms say they're looking for the 'right stuff,' they often mean an elusive combination of economic, social and cultural resources that only those from affluent backgrounds possess."

In a subsequent opinion piece in the *New York Times*, Rivera elaborated on the kinds of attributes that most readily explain who gets the best paying jobs in banking, management consulting, and law, particularly as practiced by the big, prestigious firms. Over the course of nine months, she interviewed more than 100 people who reviewed applications and conducted interviews at one particular firm. While résumés served as the first cut, determining who went forward to be interviewed, it was the interviewers' impression of "fit" that decided who was offered a job: "Fit has become a catchall used to justify hiring people who are similar to decision makers and rejecting people who are not," and, more to the point, "in many organizations, fit has gone rogue" (Rivera 2015). We do not disagree with Rivera's analysis or New's summary of her work. Quite the contrary. She nicely documents what most people interested in top-end jobs assume to be true—and it is an assumption that increases *US News & World Report* sales and swells the applicant pools of the nation's top Medallion colleges and universities.

The second article was a briefer report in *Inside Higher Ed*, summarizing the results of an Accenture survey of recent and soon-to-be college graduates in the spring of 2015, which reflected much of the confusion surrounding the role labor market data might play in the college-choice process. The awkward finding, for those inclined to argue that colleges and universities know how to prepare their students for the labor market, was that 49 percent of the students who graduated from college in 2013 and 2014 reported that they were underemployed—and one out of three recent graduates was not working at a job that matched his or her collegiate major. An even larger proportion reported that they were earning less than $25,000 annually. On the other hand, 64 percent felt that their education prepared them well for the workforce. The good news was that those who were college seniors during 2014–15 were much more upbeat. Eighty-five percent said they expected to earn more than $25,000 annually, and 80 percent reported that they believed their college education prepared them well for the workforce.

Several explanations are possible here. First, the graduates who entered the labor market in either 2013 or 2014 were still confronting the aftermath of what has come to be called the Great Recession—a time of limited employment and curtailed wages. By the spring of 2015, considerably better news was on the horizon: modest wage growth plus slowly expanding employment. The 2013 and 2014 graduates simply got there too late or too early—too late to enjoy the pre-2007 wage premiums college graduates were routinely earning, and too late to enjoy the modest rebound in American optimism. The explanation of that wide gap between the seniors in 2015 and their predecessors is that the latter's real experience with the labor market was a chilling one—not because they were unprepared for work, but because the economy did not need them at the salaries they expected to earn.

Two recent books drive home this point. The first, *The Global Auction*, by a trio of anti-Thatcherite economists—Phillip Brown, Hugh Lauder and

David Ashton—asked simply and pointedly if a knowledge-driven economy increases the demand for college-educated workers: "Will it be enough for individuals to invest in their talents and abilities as they had done in the past to secure a well-paid job via educational achievement?" The authors then go on to ask if America can succeed in garnering a "large share of the global supply of high-skill, high-wage jobs" (Brown, Lauder, and Ashton 2010, 2).

The problem is one of political expectations, where too many politicians have bought into Thomas Friedman's thesis in *The World Is Flat* (2005). What his book seemingly promised was a world with smart people doing smart things in smart ways. Learning was expected to equal earning, in an opportunity bargain that justified spending ever increasing amounts of public funds in a bid to outsmart rivals in the competition for the best jobs, technologies, and companies. The result, *The Global Auction* argues, was that affluent countries created policies and programs to support a future of "high-skill, high-wage work." This massive expansion, the authors contend, has encouraged students to incur high personal debt in order to obtain "credentials in the belief that they will be well rewarded once they enter the job market" (Brown, Lauder, and Ashton 2010, 5).

It hasn't worked out the way the optimists had hoped. The result is really a broken promise, the effects of which those in the United States are just beginning to comprehend. Americans, say the authors of *The Global Auction*, are "ill-prepared to meet the challenges posed by the new era of knowledge capitalism because they are caught in a gale of creative destruction that makes it difficult to find individual solutions to changing economic realities." They believe that both the numbers of managerial and professional jobs will be fewer than anticipated, and that "the quality of working life and rewards associated with those jobs" will be disappointing. These authors cite decades of stagnant wages for most of the college educated, excepting a select minority "who succeed in the competition for the best jobs" (Brown, Lauder, and Ashton 2010, 5).

The second sobering work is by our colleague Peter Cappelli of the Wharton School. In *Will College Pay Off? A Guide to the Most Important Financial Decision You'll Ever Make*, Cappelli (2015) sets out to make sense of a labor market that, for new entrants, is not likely to deliver on the host of promises colleges and universities make in their recruiting materials. What prompted Cappelli to join the debate was the seemingly endless flow of hype about the economic rewards of a college degree that encouraged many students to take on large amounts of debt without understanding the possibility of a poor payoff. The author laments that "while there are lots of guides to tell us whether a particular school suits the temperament of our child, there is almost nothing that helps us decide whether a college experience will lead to financial ruin" (Cappelli 2015, 3).

It is a largely dispassionate argument, stating that nothing is very certain for very long. Well-paying first jobs can easily fall victim to changing technologies and the willingness of employers to substitute lower-paid first-time workers for employees who entered the labor market a decade or more ago. Fields shift, jobs change, and the supply of college-educated workers keeps growing. It is Cappelli's broader conclusion, however, that captured our attention. He points out that a strong argument for earning a bachelor's degree is the widening wage gap between high school and college graduates. Yet he attributes this gap not to the strong salaries of college graduates, but rather to the declining wages of those without degrees. That is an important distinction, because "it could well be that college grads do far better than high school grads and still do not earn enough to pay back the cost of their college degrees." Cappelli also claims that "implicit in the arguments about this college wage premium is the notion that a high school grad would have earned what a college grad earns if only he or she had gone to college." That, he believes, is a false argument: "Kids who go on to college have many advantages over those who do not. Some of those advantages have to do with abilities, some with family background and resources that would have allowed them to do better in life even if they did not go on to college" (Cappelli 2015, 179).

We have long been suspicious of claims that producing more college graduates boosts the economy, observing instead that expanding economies create a demand for college graduates that, in turn, produces the wage premiums that college and university recruiting materials routinely promise. A surplus of college graduates educated in the wrong fields is not the problem. Rather, it is the worldwide surplus of smart, ambitious people who, as Brown, Lauder, and Ashton point out, are reducing the cost of labor through a "Dutch, or reverse, auction" that both lowers starting wages and caps continuing salaries for college-educated workers. Today's employees, they suggest, are expected to work longer hours for lower salaries, to accept inferior retirement benefits and health care coverage, and to face declining job security and limited career opportunities. These problems, once restricted to low-skills endeavors, have now encroached on fields requiring expertise, "forcing American students, workers, and families into a bare-knuckle fight for those jobs that continue to offer a good standard of living" (Brown, Lauder, and Ashton 2010, 7). The other result that these authors point to, which the young workers in the Accenture survey are just discovering, is that many of them will take jobs that really don't require a college education.

A Public Policy Deficit

We have, then, a first answer to our question, "Does it really matter?" We don't see a major mismatch between what colleges and universities offer in terms of their majors. Deficits of opportunity, when and where they occur, are principally the product of a stagnant economy, on the one hand, and, on the other, of the exaggerated promises made by policy makers and university leaders. The deficits that are particularly troubling are those reflected in the rhetoric of public officials and their policy wonk allies, who are all too ready to blame a paucity of good job information, along with overly expensive college educations, as the real culprits. While we are not at all sure that students and their parents need to know about the detailed workings of the labor market, we are certain that those responsible for public policy need to pay much more attention to the interplay between the labor market and the market for a baccalaureate education. It is a point we have made before.

In 2006, Pennsylvania's Governor's Office asked us to explore the state of higher education across the Commonwealth. The governor, we were told, was willing to substantially increase the state's support for higher education, provided that the additional monies would demonstrably yield a better economy for all Pennsylvanians. Our study yielded some of the answers the governor was looking for—in particular, a rationale for increasing the funding for the Commonwealth's system of state-owned comprehensive universities. Our report indicated that if Pennsylvania wanted to provide a technically proficient labor force that was likely remain in the state to work, then "those institutions with large in-state enrollments will have to substantially increase the number of students they graduate with degrees in math, science, computing, and engineering" (EPLC and TLA 2006, 42). We pointed out that there had been a recent decline in STEM degrees from institutions in the Pennsylvania State System of Higher Education, and that the first step was to reverse that downturn.

We wove into our narrative a real concern that those responsible for public policy did not understand how or why Pennsylvania was a net importer of the kinds of college students who were likely to pursue high-skill/high-pay jobs wherever those jobs happened to exist—which probably was not in Pennsylvania. While there had been a substantial increase in the number of graduates from Pennsylvania institutions majoring in the STEM disciplines, "most of that growth was in colleges and universities that tend to import students, institutions whose students most likely were better attuned to the national labor market than focused on opportunities in Pennsylvania" (EPLC and TLA 2006, 42). The other half of the problem, we pointed out, stemmed from Pennsylvania employers' reluctance or inability to pay the kinds of salaries that attracted these graduates. We recommended that Commonwealth employers make their jobs "more attractive by offering higher salaries, better working conditions, and more opportunities for advanced study." And we suggested that the state could take an active role by creating new graduate programs and providing additional funding for student aid.

Our cautions went unheeded. Neither the governor nor the heads of the state's institutions were very interested in targeted investments, such as those we recommended. It proved to be easier, and a lot more feasible politically, to push for better consumer information, while the political establishment, including a new governor from the opposite political party, stressed the importance of producing more college graduates while simultaneously lowering the price and, hence, the costs, associated with a baccalaureate education. What was missing then, as now, was much interest in the structure of the market for a baccalaureate education: the push/pull of a labor market that often results in the export of locally educated workers to other states, or the role lower wages play in lessening the bonus college graduates hope to achieve through their investments in higher education.

Lauren Rivera also has cautions about the value of labor market information, particularly when the focus is on the high-salaried jobs the graduates of Medallion institutions so persistently seek. Here she took to task the institutions that, for their own benefit, exaggerate the importance of rankings, particularly those based on the postgraduation earning capacities of their students. Jake New asked her, "Should colleges be concerned by the fact that the elite firms might care more about who an institution lets in than what that student gets out of the education there?" She responded that "elite universities actually have strong incentives to turn a blind eye to this. Rankings and revenues have become crucial performance metrics for universities" (New 2015). Rivera went on to say that salaries earned by recent graduates of business and law schools are factored into the rankings of their institutions. This calculus creates an incentive for those colleges and universities to place as many students as possible in high-paying jobs and to disregard why employers are interested in hiring their students.

More generally, Rivera's caution speaks to the dangers of overemphasizing the importance of employability and the variability of the labor market. It is, as we have said before, a matter of knowing the territory. The irony, from our perspective, is that students and their parents seem to know what to expect and shape their college choices accordingly. It is those responsible for the nation's higher education systems and institutions who do not know enough to make credible decisions in this regard.

5

Fifty States

Thirty years ago, Bruce Johnstone, a member of the original Pew Higher Education Roundtable and chancellor of the State University of New York (SUNY), declared that there was no United States system of higher education—no minister, as in Europe; no truly ministerial functions; but, rather, a lightly regarded Department of Education that naturally gave way to the initiatives and interests of some 50 separate state systems of education, each with its own history and regional distinctiveness. There were few truly national universities, though, ironically perhaps, presidents like Clark Kerr (University of California System), Theodore Hesburgh (University of Notre Dame), and William Friday (University of North Carolina System) were more visible as national leaders than their successors are today.

Three decades later, the federal government is now higher education's principal third-party payer, investing more than $190 billion a year in the enterprise. Federal student financial aid programs have yielded a more national methodology for distributing monetary assistance to help students to attend the college of their choice. Federal research support, whether from the National Science Foundation, the National Institutes of Health, the Department of Defense, or a host of additional federal agencies, supplies almost all of the monies that undergird the nation's investments in both basic and applied research. The growing importance of federal funds has also yielded an increased appetite on the part of the US Department of Education, along with the agencies responsible for the nation's research agendas, to impose a set of policies and regulations governing both institutional and individual behavior.

As federal initiatives have become more important, the role of the states has receded. While, collectively, the 50 states still spend more money in support of higher education than does the federal government, that support has declined significantly, relative to that federal share. More vexing has been the eclipsing of what was once a heady mix of state policies that set about shaping, often successfully, an individual state's higher education system, in the hopes of providing a greater, more equally distributed set of opportunities that would also spur economic development. California, with its Master Plan for Higher Education, was the best known and most widely imitated of these mega-experiments in state policy making.

A Growing Absence of Big Ideas

Predating Kerr's efforts to create a layered system of interconnected institutions across California, however, was the Wisconsin Idea, which was a product of that state's long engagement with progressive reforms. At its core, the Idea was a partnership between state government and its public university (the University of Wisconsin) to make good on the promise of better government, or, as President Theodore Roosevelt would note in the introduction to the book that came to define the Idea: "In Wisconsin there has been a successful effort to redeem . . . promises by performances, and to reduce theories into practice" (Roosevelt 1912).

Initially, the Wisconsin Idea established the roles the state's university system and, more particularly, its faculty would play in shaping the public initiatives that came to define the state's progressivism. One observer noted that faculty members served on a broad variety of advisory boards and applied their expertise to help guide the state's administration. Thus the Idea underscored the universities' historic commitment to public service. By the 1930s, a university publication described the Idea by stating, "The boundaries of campus are the boundaries of the state." The spirit of the Wisconsin Idea persists today and "has become the guiding philosophy of university outreach efforts in Wisconsin and throughout the world" (UW–Madison 2017).

In the 1950s and 1960s, North Carolina became the model for those who advocated investing in higher education as a precondition to economic development. Two governors defined the approach: Luther Hodges, who later became secretary of commerce, and his gubernatorial successor,

Terry Sanford, who would later become a US senator after first serving for 16 years as president of Duke University. Both were advocates of what might best be called an "if we build it, they will come" policy of funding specific investments in higher education, as a means of luring northern and midwestern industries to North Carolina. It was a set of policy initiatives that stressed across-the-board investments: in K–12 education, as well as in colleges, universities, community colleges, and the Research Triangle (linking the University of North Carolina, North Carolina State University, and Duke University). North Carolina's promise to businesses was one of guaranteeing an educated workforce for those firms that relocated all or part of their enterprises in the state. Included in that promise was the guarantee that the state's community colleges would provide job-specific training at little or no cost to the firms.

Each of these grand notions—California's Master Plan, the Wisconsin Idea, and the North Carolina Promise—today are icons of a bygone era, as much forgotten as they are misremembered. California, it turned out, was too big, too complex, and too politically and ethnically diverse to maintain an integrated system of higher education that hewed closely to Kerr's original vision. North Carolina is similarly more complex and, frankly, more economically successful, to need the full complement of programs that were once integral to the North Carolina Promise. The Wisconsin Idea is now in tatters—the victim of near-open warfare launched by a Republican governor with presidential ambitions, who has made the faculty of the University of Wisconsin System not partners, but targets of enmity.

More generally, state-initiated policies for funding and developing a state's system of higher education have lost political traction. State *policy* has been replaced by *reactions*—for the most part, short-term initiatives designed to solve a particular problem, most often occasioned by a budget shortfall or a major shift in political alliances. Arizona has probably been the most aggressive in cutting state support for higher education, all the while adopting some of the same mean-spiritedness that has come to characterize the political clashes in Wisconsin.

Most state actions, however, have been largely devoid of ideology—as well as good ideas. What transpired in Iowa in the spring of 2015 is typical. The state's Board of Regents sought to ensure additional enrollment and, hence, revenue for the University of Northern Iowa. Its solution was to craft a funding program based mostly on enrollments—in essence creating a financial incentive for the University of Iowa and Iowa State University, in addition to the University of Northern Iowa, to increase their recruitment of in-state students. There was never any announced intention to redistribute enrollments, though that was exactly what happened. For the fall of 2015, only a few of Iowa's private colleges and universities met their planned enrollment goals for first-time, full-time students. Alas, the story doesn't end there. It turned out that the Board of Regents did not have the authority to change the funding formula. It could recommend actions, but only the state legislature could enact them. The legislature, however, had little interest in what the regents proposed and left the old funding formula in place. The result was significantly enlarged first-year classes at Iowa, Iowa State, and Northern Iowa—but no increase in state funding. And it was too late for the public universities to turn off the spigot, or for the private colleges that had lower enrollments to recoup their losses. The result: everyone lost, including the Board of Regents.

The States as Market Markers

The significance of these state actions is a reminder of the importance of states in the functioning of the market for undergraduate education across the nation. But instead of 50 separate systems linked by tradition and a few truly national universities—some private, like Harvard, Yale, Princeton, and Stanford; and some public, like Michigan, UC Berkeley, Wisconsin, and Virginia—what has emerged is an amalgamation of different perspectives and traditions, each compelled to come to terms with the increasing federalization of funding for student financial aid and the dynamics of a marketplace that stresses competitiveness at almost any cost.

One way to understand the importance of the states in the functioning of the market for undergraduate education is to focus on the distribution of enrollments across the major sectors for a sample of representative states. Figure 5.1 graphs those distributions for California, Massachusetts, New Jersey, and New Mexico. The dissimilarities are truly striking. California's Master Plan for Higher Education of more than a half century ago has resulted in a robust community college sector in that state. In sharp contrast, the Two-Year sector in Massachusetts accounts for only 20 percent of that state's 290,000 FTE enrollments. Instead, its historic tradition of private institutions, dating back to the colonial era, helps explain why a

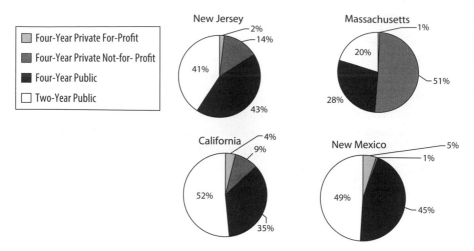

Figure 5.1. Distribution of FTE degree-seeking students

majority of its FTE degree seekers enroll in the Four-Year Private Not-for-Profit sector, while in New Mexico, with 89,000 FTE degree seekers, that sector is almost nonexistent. All four states have a Four-Year Public presence, but while well over 40 percent of New Mexico's and New Jersey's FTE degree seekers enroll in that sector, fewer than 30 percent of Massachusetts' enrollments are found there. For-Profit institutions garner just a sliver of enrollments in the two East Coast states and make a slightly greater showing in the West Coast ones.

At the same time, our analysis, based on IPEDS' 2012 data on the home residency of first-time, full-time enrollees, finds that there is a substantial movement of students between states. This phenomenon occurs in all eight regions of the country. The top seven net importing states are located in seven different regions, while the seven largest net exporters are found in six different ones.

There are striking differences among the 50 states on two fronts: the sheer numbers of first-time, full-time students leaving or entering a particular state, and the variety of import to export patterns (table 5.1). The state with the largest number of net imports was Arizona, with more than 22,000. Nearly 26,800 first-time, full-time students from other states enrolled in Arizona institutions, while only 4,691 Arizonans sought their educations elsewhere. On the opposite end of the spectrum, New Jersey

Table 5.1. State net imports and exports, all institutions

State	Imports less exports	Import/ export ratio
Arizona	22,103	5.7
Pennsylvania	16,084	1.9
Iowa	11,748	4.6
West Virginia	10,936	8.2
Massachusetts	8,952	1.5
Indiana	8,621	2.2
Florida	8,541	1.5
Alabama	7,120	2.4
Utah	7,066	5.3
District of Columbia	6,491	3.9
New York	5,897	1.2
Rhode Island	5,777	3.1
Missouri	5,251	1.7
Virginia	5,198	1.4
South Carolina	4,989	2.1
Oklahoma	4,424	2.6
North Carolina	3,788	1.4
Ohio	3,231	1.2
North Dakota	3,126	4.3
Vermont	2,876	2.3
Kentucky	2,856	1.7
Arkansas	2,764	2.1
Wisconsin	2,632	1.3
Oregon	2,496	1.5
New Hampshire	1,687	1.3
Louisiana	1,537	1.4
Idaho	1,534	1.6
South Dakota	1,513	2.1
Delaware	1,483	1.7
Colorado	1,305	1.2
Montana	1,111	1.9
Michigan	1,106	1.1
Kansas	1,037	1.3
Nebraska	754	1.3
Maine	697	1.2
Tennessee	473	1.1
Mississippi	393	1.1
Wyoming	(22)	1.0
New Mexico	(39)	1.0
Alaska	(554)	0.62
Hawaii	(1,574)	0.51
Nevada	(1,743)	0.48
Washington	(2,774)	0.71
Minnesota	(4,523)	0.66
Connecticut	(5,219)	0.65
Georgia	(5,422)	0.67

(continued)

Table 5.1. (*continued*)

State	Imports less exports	Import/ export ratio
Maryland	(9,255)	0.46
California	(14,445)	0.60
Texas	(14,687)	0.40
Illinois	(15,615)	0.50
New Jersey	(28,727)	0.15

exported nearly 34,000 of its residents to other states as first-year, first-time students but imported fewer than 5,000, claiming the smallest import to export ratio, at barely 0.15. West Virginia had the largest import to export ratio, 8.2, importing 12,457 first-year, full-time students to institutions in its state in 2012, while only 1,521 of its residents enrolled out of state—an import surplus of nearly 11,000.

What these differences reflect are the varying choices available to students and their families, depending on the state in which they live—and whether or not they are prepared to enroll in a college or university outside their state. While the overall shape, and even the structure, of the market is national in scope, and the distinct roles the segments play relative to one another are as described in chapters 1 and 2, there remain important local variations that state political leaders fail to understand, at their own peril. One of the key differences involves the average market prices charged in various states by Four-Year Public and Four-Year Private Not-for-Profit institutions. Figure 5.2 plots the average market prices for Four-Year Public versus Private Not-for-Profit institutions in each of the 50 states. The upper-right quadrant, dominated by states located in the Northeast (New England and the Middle Atlantic region), displays the states where both Public and Private average market prices are above the median for the United States. In contrast, the lower-left quadrant, noticeably lacking most states in the Northeast or the West, contains states where prices are lower in both sectors. The remaining two quadrants plot where the Public/Private prices are high and low (*lower right*), or low and high (*upper left*).

Two important conclusions can be drawn from this display. First, there is wide variance in the average market prices across the 50 states. In 2012, Four-Year Public market prices ranged from the lowest (just over $4,000), in Mississippi, to just over $14,000 in Delaware, at the high end. The range

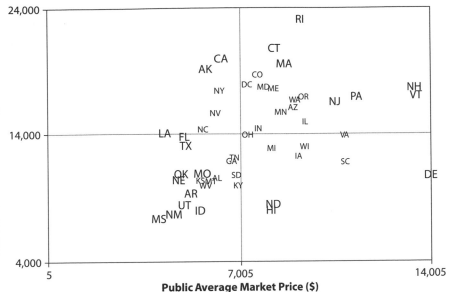

Figure 5.2. Average statewide market prices for Four-Year Public and Four-Year Private Not-for-Profit institutions

in average market prices charged by Four-Year Private Not-for-Profit colleges and universities across states was even greater. The lowest state average market price was again that of Mississippi, at just over $7,400. The highest—almost $16,000 more than Mississippi's—was in Rhode Island (at $23,122), largely reflecting the costly prices of institutions such as Brown University and the Rhode Island School of Design.

In a bicoastal nation, in which the edges are culturally as well as economically and ethnically different from the nation's heartland, it should not be surprising that New England and the Middle Atlantic states, along with the West Coast, have noticeably higher average market prices—particularly in the Private sector. Besides Rhode Island, Connecticut (with institutions such as Yale and Wesleyan Universities), California (with the likes of Stanford University, the University of Southern California, the California Institute of Technology, and Pomona College), and Massachusetts (including Harvard University, the Massachusetts Institute of Technology, Tufts University, Boston University, and Boston College) claim the highest market prices in the Private sector.

The second finding is that there is great variance among states in the gap between the average Four-Year Public and Four-Year Private Not-for-Profit prices. Figure 5.2 reflects both the geographic distribution of high-priced Medallion institutions and the ability of some state cultures to hold down the price of a college education. California is perhaps the best example: its private institutions have among the highest average market prices, while its Public colleges and universities fall below the national median.

Two 50-State Roll Calls

Gaining a graphic perspective on state practices and proclivities is not as easy as graphing the impact of sectors and segments on the market for undergraduate education. There are simply too many states, too many variables, and too much variance. What follows is an attempt to put in summary form the principal differences among the state systems of higher education. We offer a pair of indices summarizing the key measures for slicing and dicing the market developed in chapter 3.

The first index focuses on the demographic diversity of the Four-Year Public institutions in each state, in terms of four basic attributes:

- the percentage of degree-seeking undergraduates who are Nonwhite (NW);
- the percentage of undergraduates with Pell Grants (PL);
- the percentage of undergraduates who are 25 years or older (≥25); and
- the percentage of undergraduates who attend part time (PT).

In table 5.2, we classified the roll call of states according to the number (zero to all four) of attributes that are at or above the 67th percentile—that is, the number of attributes for which those states are in the top third of each distribution. Here, it is important to note that what is being reported are *institutional* averages. We have ordered each set according to the average institutional market price for each state for its Four-Year Public colleges and universities, although market price did not contribute to each state's overall diversity score. As you peruse the patterns reflected in table 5.2, some conclusions are more readily apparent than others. For example, of the four states with the most diverse (on average) institutions, not one is in the New England, Middle Atlantic, or West Coast regions. Two of those states are former members of the Confederate States of America.

Table 5.2. Measures of institutional diversity: Four-Year Public institutions across all 50 states

State	Market price ($)	Attributes ≥67th percentile*
Most Diverse		
New Mexico	4,590	all
Texas	5,065	all
Alabama	5,906	all
Illinois	9,394	all
Diverse		
Mississippi	4,093	NW ≥25 PL
Alaska	5,817	NW ≥25 PT
Nevada	6,122	NW ≥25 PT
Hawaii	8,105	NW ≥25 PT
Somewhat Diverse		
Louisiana	4,295	NW PT
Oklahoma	4,743	PL ≥25
Utah	4,990	≥25 PT
Florida	5,004	PL PT
Idaho	5,554	PL ≥25
North Carolina	5,674	NW PL
Montana	5,993	PL ≥25
California	6,334	NW PL
Georgia	6,677	NW PL
Maryland	7,847	NW ≥25
Maine	8,251	≥25 PT
Oregon	9,335	≥25 PT
New Jersey	10,464	NW ≥25
Not Very Diverse		
Arkansas	5,238	PL
Kansas	5,625	PT
West Virginia	5,786	PL
New York	6,270	NW
Tennessee	6,798	PL
South Dakota	6,841	PT
Ohio	7,281	PL
Indiana	7,657	PT
Connecticut	8,265	PT
Delaware	14,003	NW
Not Diverse		
Nebraska	4,814	none
Missouri	5,624	none
Kentucky	6,942	none
Wyoming	7,328	none
Colorado	7,655	none
Michigan	8,140	none
North Dakota	8,167	none
Minnesota	8,486	none

(continued)

Table 5.2. (*continued*)

State	Market price ($)	Attributes ≥67th percentile*
Massachusetts	8,619	none
Arizona	8,939	none
Washington	9,012	none
Iowa	9,138	none
Rhode Island	9,217	none
Wisconsin	9,371	none
Virginia	10,839	none
South Carolina	10,856	none
Pennsylvania	11,265	none
Vermont	13,435	none
New Hampshire	13,498	none

*Attributes at or above the 67th percentile: NW=percentage of Nonwhites; PL=percentage with Pell Grants; ≥25=percentage age 25 or older; PT=percentage of Part-Time.

At the same time, market price is something of a proxy for diversity. Within the eight most-diverse states, only two have an average market price that is higher than the median ($7,328) for the full set of 50 states. On the other hand, of the 19 states with the least diverse set of Public colleges and universities, all but three have higher average market prices than the median.

Our second index focused on what we have called "competitive advantage," based on our analysis of market sectors and segments (table 5.3). We used just three attributes, ones that reflect almost perfectly the structure of the market expressed in terms of the Medallion through Convenience segments. We noted the number of attributes in which the state averages for Four-Year Publics scored in the top third of the nation:

- six-year graduation rate (GR);
- percentage of STEM majors (SM); and
- average faculty salaries (FS).

In many ways the roll call of states focusing on competitive advantage is the complement of the one featuring demographic diversity. Of the 20 least-advantaged states, eight (40 percent) had average institutional market prices above the median. The five most-advantaged states included two expected powerhouses—Michigan and California—and two surprises, Arizona and Wyoming. Of these five, four states had average market prices above the median, with one (California) below it.

Table 5.3. Measures of competitive advantage: Four-Year Public institutions across all 50 states

State	Market price ($)	Attributes ≥67th percentile*
Most advantaged		
Iowa	9,138	all
Arizona	8,939	all
Michigan	8,140	all
Wyoming	7,328	all
California	6,334	all
Advantaged		
Delaware	14,003	GR FS
Virginia	10,839	GR FS
New Jersey	10,464	GR FS
Wisconsin	9,371	GR SM
Rhode Island	9,217	GR FS
Massachusetts	8,619	GR FS
Connecticut	8,265	GR FS
Maryland	7,847	SM FS
New York	6,270	GR FS
Modestly advantaged		
New Hampshire	13,498	GR
Washington	9,012	GR
Maine	8,251	SM
Hawaii	8,105	FS
Colorado	7,655	SM
South Dakota	6,841	SM
Georgia	6,677	SM
Nevada	6,122	FS
Montana	5,993	SM
Alaska	5,817	SM
West Virginia	5,786	SM
North Carolina	5,674	GR
Missouri	5,624	SM
Texas	5,065	FS
Florida	5,004	GR
New Mexico	4,590	SM
Not advantaged		
Vermont	13,435	none
Pennsylvania	11,265	none
South Carolina	10,856	none
Illinois	9,394	none
Oregon	9,335	none
Minnesota	8,486	none
North Dakota	8,167	none
Indiana	7,657	none
Ohio	7,281	none
Kentucky	6,942	none

(continued)

Table 5.3. (*continued*)

State	Market price ($)	Attributes ≥67th percentile*
Tennessee	6,798	none
Alabama	5,906	none
Kansas	5,625	none
Idaho	5,554	none
Arkansas	5,238	none
Utah	4,990	none
Nebraska	4,814	none
Oklahoma	4,743	none
Louisiana	4,295	none
Mississippi	4,093	none

*Attributes at or above the 67th percentile: GR=graduation rate; SM= percentage of STEM majors; FS=faculty salaries.

Table 5.4. Demographic diversity and competitive advantage: Four-Year Public institutions

	Most advantaged or advantaged	Modestly or not advantaged
Most diverse, diverse, or somewhat diverse	3	18
Not very or not diverse	11	18

A simple, four-fold table (table 5.4), combining the two indices of state-by-state demographic diversity and competitive advantage provides a quick summary. The findings are simple and straightforward: the most advantaged institutions are among the less diverse (11 out of 14), and among the states that, on average, have more-diverse colleges and universities, only three can be said to be competitively advantaged.

Variances in Market Structure

Like the distribution of sectors discussed at the outset of this chapter, the distribution of market segments varies widely from state to state. Figure 5.3 depicts the segment distributions for both Private Not-for-Profit and Four-Year Public institutions in six states. Each state is relatively well populated and each, by tradition, has a strong complement of both Public and Private Not-for-Profit institutions. On the Public side of the ledger,

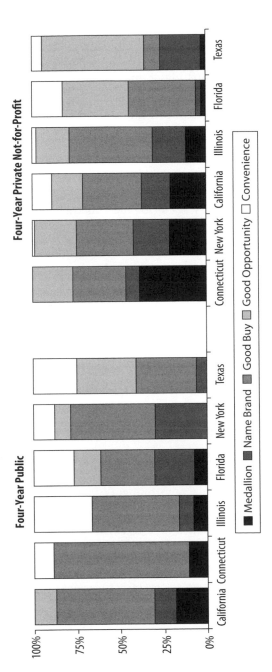

Figure 5.3. Distribution of segments across six sample states

California provides an advantageous selection of colleges and universities, thanks, in part, to the competitive strength of the University of California System: six Medallions, two Name Brands, and one Good Buy, the new campus at Merced. Texas and New York are without Medallions: neither the University of Texas at Austin nor any of the SUNY campuses meet the six-year graduation rate standard. Nonetheless, both of these states, along with containing a selection of Good Buy and Good Opportunity schools, house strong Name Brand institutions—the University of Texas at Austin and Texas A&M University's main campus (in College Station) in the former, and a number of SUNY campuses, including at Binghamton and Buffalo, in the latter. Only Florida boasts Public institutions in every market segment, with the University of Florida meeting the Medallion criterion.

The distribution of the five segments across the Four-Year Private Not-for-Profit sector is quite different. Connecticut is home to five Medallion institutions, and Florida and Texas have but one each. Almost half of the Four-Year Private Not-for-Profit colleges and universities in Illinois are Good Buys. In Texas, the single largest group is in the Good Opportunity sector: lower cost, not as selective, and, in terms of graduation rates, less successful. Thus what might work as good state policy in Connecticut will necessarily be different from that in Texas or Florida. At the same time, what works on the Public side of the ledger might not be so successful on the Private side.

Gaining Perspective

A half century ago, if you wanted to know the status of higher education in America in general, and, in particular, the kinds of policies that created good educational environments, you had only to look to the states. Clark Kerr and California's Master Plan were the exemplars everyone knew about and most states tried to emulate, in one form or another. Several generations of higher education researchers and policy wonks began with the assumption that changing higher education for the better meant revising how the states, particularly those with growing Public sector systems, went about the process of setting goals and appropriating funds.

At the close of the twentieth century, the notion that state policies and practices held the key to reforming American higher education had champions everywhere. The most astute, as well as the most influential, was Patrick Callan, a policy wonk's policy wonk, whose résumé reads like a road map on how to shape state policy by influencing state policy makers. By 1991, when he established the Higher Education Policy Institute (an independent, nonprofit, nonpartisan organization), Callan had already served as vice president of the Education Commission of the States; had founded and led the California Higher Education Policy Center and then the National Center for Public Policy and Higher Education (NCPPHE); had served as executive director of state higher education boards and commissions in Montana, Washington, and California, and as staff director of the California legislature's Joint Committee on the Master Plan for Higher Education; and was, like Bruce Johnstone, a founding member of the Pew Higher Education Roundtable. It was in his capacity as NCPPHE's head that Callan led the development of the biannual, 50-state scorecard, *Measuring Up*, which that center first issued in 2000.

Measuring Up reflected two core precepts jointly held by Callan and his political partner, Governor John Hunt of North Carolina. The first belief held that measurements leading to meaningful comparisons were important. Governor Hunt said it best in declaring that "the things we keep track of, count, and monitor tend to be the ones we improve" (NCPPHE 2000, 9). He went on to say that a state-by-state report card provides public officials with a yardstick to measure "higher education performance and opportunity across states" and supplies sets of standards across a series of higher education objectives: from affordability to access to completions, to name a few.

The second core belief held that the nation's 50 states were to be the prime movers in assuring that all citizens could benefit from the nation's investments in its colleges and universities, and in providing an educated workforce capable of maintaining the United States' economic standing. Callan described this tenet as one recognizing that states are principally responsible for public policy in education. He wrote that states prepare students for college, and they "provide most of the direct financial support to—and oversight of—public colleges and universities and give significant direct and indirect support to private ones through student financial aid, tax exemptions and, in some instances, direct appropriations" (NCPPHE 2000, 12). He went on to argue that the states are the architects of public higher education, and that it is states that can foster coordination between K–12 and higher education, as well as between Public and Private higher education sectors: "Federal initiatives are significant, but only the states have the means and the broad responsibility for ensuring opportunity for education, training and retraining beyond high school."

The final 50-state report card for which Hunt and Callan bore principal responsibility was issued in 2008. It could boast of having spurred some changes, but, at heart, the message in *Measuring Up 2008* was more somber, more like a jeremiad. Hunt, lamenting the nation's disparity in opportunity and success, put the matter squarely: "Family wealth and income, race and ethnicity, and geography play too great a role in determining which Americans receive a high school education that prepares them for college, which ones enroll in college, and which ones complete certificate or degree programs." Callan's essay was blunter, with a title that left no doubt that the battle for a responsive system of higher education was yet to be won: "Modest Improvements, Persistent Disparities, Eroding Global Competitiveness" (NCPPHE 2008, 4–5).

Measuring Up 2008 was equally candid about the continued absence of a real set of metrics for measuring progress. Much of the statistical evidence undergirding each edition of *Measuring Up* had been developed by the National Center for Higher Education Management Systems (NCHEMS) and its president, Dennis Jones. In this final *Measuring Up*, Jones awarded a grade of F to the nation's effort to develop and collect good comparative indicators for higher education. He bemoaned the lack of real progress in building a reliable, as well as robust, national information system. Despite early attempts in *Measuring Up* to identify the key areas where state-by-state metrics were needed, the data remained deficient. Jones blamed the lack of participation by some states, as well as the failure of national organizations to press for sufficient data from the states (NCPPHE 2008, 20).

Although the National Center for Public Policy and Higher Education has closed, and *Measuring Up 2008* remains without a successor, much of the overall policy analysis in higher education remains state centered— and the analyses themselves are more somber, less certain that success is at hand. Among the best of these efforts is that of our colleagues Laura Perna and Joni Finney. Their *Attainment Agenda* (2014), with a foreword by Callan, continues to argue that the impetus for reforms necessarily remains centered in the 50 states.

After considerable reflection, we have taken a different tack. We see little reason to be optimistic about prospects for meaningful change or reform being driven by state initiatives. Ironically, perhaps, one of the items we reviewed in preparing to write this chapter was a 2014 op-ed article by Finney and Callan, arguing that it was past the time for California to revise its Master Plan for Higher Education. There was a new bluntness to their message that could hardly be missed: "The most fundamental failure has been the unwillingness on the part of state and higher education leaders to reexamine assumptions that were embodied in the 1960 Master Plan for Higher Education" (Finney and Callan 2014). They went on to say that California, once a national leader in higher education, had fallen below the national average in sending its high school graduates directly on to college. Callan and Finney lamented the failure of California to revisit its "historic blueprint for higher education," even though the state's population had quadrupled and the global economy had been transformed. At the same time, the state had reduced its "capacity for policy, oversight and public accountability." The authors noted that all this resulted in California facing a shortage of the college-educated and skilled workers it needed to meet the economy's future challenges.

This situation exists not just in California, but everywhere. Budgetary survival has become the only policy that matters, along with a persistent mantra that taxes need to be cut; tuition prices at state-owned colleges and universities must become cheaper; and faculty, at best, are a necessary inconvenience. Look, for example, at the continuing ebb and flow of experiments with performance-based funding. Much to-do always accompanies their enactment, and then little or nothing changes. A short notice in the spring of 2015 in the *Chronicle of Higher Education* serves as a monument to the futility of most state policy making today. Two Michigan public universities announced that they would not limit their tuition increases to the 3.2 percent needed to qualify for the performance bonus required "by a governor and lawmakers eager to score political points" (*CHE* 2015). Instead, the two universities went ahead with their planned 8 percent tuition increases, having calculated that the "money they'd get from the extra tuition . . . was about 10 times what they'd forfeit in performance-based funding as a consequence of exceeding the state's cap on tuition increases."

At this point, a little benign neglect on the part of state policy makers might be helpful, given the eagerness with which federal policy makers have sought to impose new regulations on the nation's colleges and universities. It would help immeasurably if policy makers at both the state and federal levels better understood the workings of the markets that shape the enterprises they are trying to change. We will return to this theme in chapter 7, after first exploring how and why faculty are being marginalized, as much by the market as by a political process that doesn't take into account how that market distributes students and, hence, revenues.

6

Faculty

In our earlier chapters, we explored the ways in which institutions varied across market segments economically and culturally—in terms of market price, student demographics, student attendance patterns, and curricular offerings. Now we ask how faculty characteristics play out in this segmented enterprise. We do so in a time of changing roles and expectations—even upheaval—for faculty in terms of their responsibilities and their relationship with the academy. A widely held and oft-repeated axiom is that changing American higher education is the purview of the faculty. Their business, they will tell you, is teaching and research—joint products in which the former proceeds from the latter. The best faculty are scholarly pedagogues, teaching through both example and precept what their research and their disciplines have taught them.

In theory, at least, faculty acting collaboratively and collectively ought to own the curriculum—just as certainly as each faculty member is responsible for his or her courses and research. It is this sense of shared responsibility that makes the academy what it is: somehow both a part of and yet still separate from the world. The problem is that faculty today have largely declined to play a transformative role. Too often they have responded to calls for change by arguing that what is not demonstrably broken doesn't need fixing. "Where," they wonder, "is the proof that change is necessary?" Above all, they ask: "Why now? Why not later, when the economy has been fully restored to health, when the disruptions of the present moment have faded, and when there can be more certainty about the true value and sustainability of the fixes being so hotly debated?" These are the kinds of faculty encamped just north of Armageddon. They can look over the ridge and see the destruction that awaits if they foolishly charge headlong in pursuit of change. While there are faculty members who believe, often ardently, that they must recapture the initiative to ensure that the academy is not distorted beyond recognition, most simply worry less about that which they cannot control, while saying, with increased conviction, "I think I'll sit this one out."

It is that sense of disassociation that Henry Rosovsky, then ending his second stint as dean, lamented in 1991 in his closing report to Harvard University's Faculty of Arts and Sciences. What had been lost, he told his colleagues, was the sense of a "social contract" that once bound them to one another, as well as to the institution they served. Instead, he warned, the academy "has become a society largely without rules, or to put it slightly differently, the tenured members of the faculty—frequently as individuals—make their own rules. . . . When it concerns our more important obligations—faculty citizenship—neither rule nor custom is any longer compelling" (Rosovsky 1991, 2B). Perhaps the most visible sign of the times, he told his colleagues, was a decline in just how often Harvard faculty were actually in the classroom, along with the failure of those responsible for managing the curriculum to even know what was happening. More troubling, though even harder to document, was the sense that too often the faculty were simply absent, not involved, or not engaged in the full work of the university.

Rosovsky was an insider's insider, a much-admired scholar and academic leader laying bare a set of concerns that were beginning to trouble those outside the academy as much as they discomforted the dean himself. Long gone is that somewhat bemused, mostly genteel portrait of faculty, and their college communities as places filled with interesting though often impractical scholars who are seemingly out of touch with the real world. Discarded as well are public celebrations of the life of the mind, along with the sense that scholars and the results of their learnedness are important in their own right, worthy of the public attention they once garnered. Today, faculty are most often caricatured as being a part of the problem: secure and well-compensated professionals intent on protecting their own interests at the expense of the colleges and universities they inhabit. And their institutions are, as often as not, portrayed as wasteful agencies, too often producing students with the wrong skills and attitudes for an increasingly competitive international economy.

A World Not of Our Making

An attempt to destroy the Wisconsin Idea serves as a telling example. Scott Walker, Wisconsin's Republican governor (with presidential ambitions), and a Republican-controlled legislature sought to discard the key elements of the Wisconsin Idea that once linked university faculty, state agencies, and citizens in a partnership, ensuring that knowledge created at the university was readily available to solve societal problems. Embedded in the Wisconsin Idea was the protection of the faculty by a tenure system ensconced in state statute. The governor's 2011 attack on public-service unions was followed in 2015 with a proposed budget that included a draconian $350 million reduction in state support for Wisconsin's public university system. Even worse, it included legislative language that removed the state's guarantee of tenure and changed the parameters under which faculty could be dismissed from the system's universities. Moreover, the message accompanying the submission of this budget sought to redefine the basic mission of the University of Wisconsin System, making as its principal purpose the preparation of its graduates for the workplace.

Not surprisingly, the system's faculty erupted. They produced often-elegant statements in defense of academic freedom and presented veiled threats, claiming that passing the budget and its policy pronouncements would lead to a mass exodus of the system's top scholars and grant-getters. Yet what became the focus of those outside the academy—as well as of some inside it—was the near-toxic rhetoric that spewed forth, including a number of Twitter postings from one of the University of Wisconsin–Madison's best-known sociologists, comparing the governor with Adolph Hitler and wondering whether students planning to attend that institution ought to think about making other plans.

None of it mattered very much. The budget cut was reduced from $350 million to $250 million and the rewriting of the university system's mission was glossed over when the governor's staff reported that it was all a "drafting error." By and large, the governor and his Republican legislative leaders refrained from rhetorical flourishes of their own. Walker was quoted as saying that faculty members might want to think about teaching an extra course or two and that colleges should focus more on job training and less on the humanities. But in general, the comments from his side were mostly low key: "Our plan is based on growth and opportunity, which leads to freedom and prosperity for all. . . . Secondly, our plan will use common sense reforms to create a government that is limited in scope and, ultimately, more effective, more efficient, and more accountable to the public" (Bauer 2015).

The lessons this Wisconsin imbroglio teaches are probably best reflected in how Wisconsin's regional campuses absorbed the drastic reductions in state funding imposed by the governor and the legislature. The University of Wisconsin–Eau Claire, located 180 miles northwest of Madison, is among the most beautiful of the system's campuses and is home to more than 10,000 students. It has a long tradition of liberal arts education and, in 2014, had its first Rhodes Scholar.

UW–Eau Claire received $22.1 million in state funds for 2015, as part of its $82.2 million operating budget. A year earlier, the state had supplied $29.8 million in support of this campus's operating budget of $95 million. To deal with the 25 percent loss in state support, the university principally cut costs by eliminating positions: in all, an 11 percent reduction in university employees. UW–Eau Claire's chancellor, James Schmidt, told the community: "In many ways a cut of this size feels like a betrayal from Wisconsin. . . . It also feels like a death in the family."

The chancellor's goal, as he told *Inside Higher Ed*'s Kellie Woodhouse, was to keep the reductions "as far away from the academic enterprise as possible." And that is exactly what UW–Eau Claire did. In addition to cutting its administrative staff by upward of 125 positions, this institution now has fewer midlevel officers, eliminating 7 out of 28 jobs "with titles like associate dean or vice chancellor." A major reengineering of the university's central organization—flattening it by removing many of the "silos" that had come to dominate the university's administrative apparatus—made those reductions possible. A number of centralized service centers were created, including a one-stop student services center, dealing with such functions as financial aid, registration, dining and housing contracts, and parking fees—all of which were formerly handled by separate offices at different locations. Scattered student-advising offices were consolidated into one locale, and a new administrative center covered such widely dispersed tasks as expenditures and purchasing, promising a 20 percent reduction in employees. "We had to figure out what we are going to stop doing," Schmidt explained. "How are you going to do the work differently?" (Woodhouse 2015).

Throughout this reengineering process, the faculty were kept informed, consulted at key decision points, and, above all, protected. Faculty vacancies were left unfilled, and the equivalent of 20 full-time lecturer positions were not renewed, but the core faculty and—just as importantly—the heart of the undergraduate curriculum remained as before. While average class sizes would increase slightly as a result of the unfilled faculty lecturer posts, the overall teaching load remained at four courses a semester. Though the administrative structure of the university was being redesigned, the same could not be said of the academic side of the house. No doubt the state's Republican legislators wished it otherwise, but their 2015 budget and its assault on faculty prerogatives did not result in a spasm of disruptive innovation. As the chair of UW–Eau Claire's Faculty Senate stated to Woodhouse, "We're doing the best we can to maintain the integrity of our academic program, our mission, but at least for the next couple of years there will be some challenges for students." The chair of the Political Science Department offered a more general assessment of the situation: "We don't deal well with change."

The real concern was about the fire next time. Having first noted that he and his faculty colleagues brainstormed every day about how best to get their message to the state's legislators, the chair of the Faculty Senate asked how they could "change the narrative in the capital" to prevent the same problems in the next budget cycle. He went on to warn of dire consequences—wholesale departmental closures across the University of Wisconsin System—if the budget cuts were repeated. "That's where you start to have real problems . . . real bloodletting" (Woodhouse 2015).

Faculty as Victims

Much of the narrative that has emerged from the faculty side of this dispute has focused on its members and their university campuses as victims—victims of a politically ambitious governor and a coterie of Republican legislative leaders bent on taking the University of Wisconsin System and its Madison flagship down a notch or two. What was true across Wisconsin in 2015 has become commonplace throughout much of the nation: most faculty narratives today embrace the language of victimization to counter being belittled by a public discourse that has little or no appreciation for what academics do, how hard they work, or how important their teaching and scholarship is to the life of the nation. Faculty see themselves as plagued by political processes that no longer fund universities characterized by critical thinking and the integrity of reasoned inquiry. An economic malaise has made jobs for graduates the new metric of accountability, as opposed to the virtues of scholarship and academic rigor. At the same time, faculty view themselves as the victims of shifts within the academy itself that have made their opinions less important in the running of their universities.

Not as well recognized, often by either faculty or their critics, are the workings of an academic labor market that now more readily rewards the few at the expense of the many. Faculty members, like workers everywhere, have seen the perks of those at the top of the industry greatly expanded—more money, increased independence, enhanced security—while the great majority have wages that have increased minimally if at all. They are required to do more work, with greater regulation of their time and effort, and there are further demands that they play a larger, more direct role in the recruitment and retention of students.

But mostly, faculty across the spectrum of institutions see themselves as being victimized by a market that disparages traditional scholarship and true liberal learning. The commercialization of the academy is nearly complete—jobs, not education, matter most. The competition for funds within any given college or university results in an unseemly scramble for money, and the collective ethos that "we are all in this together" becomes nearly impossible to sustain. In rhetoric, this problem is defined as commodification, best explained as the process by which markets transform educational experiences into educational commodities, or products. It is what Andrew Delbanco (2007) had in mind when he lamented that the modern university has now come dangerously close to becoming "just another corporation."

The fundamental problem, however, is not that the preponderance of faculty do not like or trust the market, but rather that most do not understand the markets that now govern so much of their lives. Because they have too often and too easily dismissed these markets as fundamentally wrongheaded, faculty are now substantially at risk. What they don't know can genuinely harm them.

What the Numbers Tell Us

We have filled the pages of this volume with what most faculty don't know—that there is a highly compartmentalized market for higher education enrollments where competitive advantage and financial reward go hand in hand. Yet it is that partitioning that shapes the context faculty will need to embrace if they intend to be in the forefront of the reform efforts now changing the lives they will lead well into the next decade.

For both Four-Year Private Not-for-Profit and Four-Year Public colleges and universities, market price goes a long way toward explaining the compensation full-time faculty receive (table 6.1). The correlation between price and faculty salaries is strong in the Private Not-for-Profit sector and more modest among the Four-Year Public colleges and universities (with correlation coefficients of 0.67 and 0.45, respectively). Only among the nation's Two-Year Public institutions is there almost no correlation (0.12) between market price and full-time faculty compensation.

Over the last several years, we have shown scatter plots of price versus salaries to a variety of faculty groups. There is always a pause, and then a kind of "OK, I get it" reaction. The more challenged an institution is in terms of enrollment, the quicker its faculty come to accept the importance of our graph. What strikes us most, however, is that at Four-Year Public colleges and universities, the tracks of faculty salaries and market price are similar, an indication of the diminishing importance of state policies and appropriations.

Table 6.1. Faculty salaries and market prices

Sector	Correlation coefficient of faculty salaries vs. market price	Mean market price ($)*	Mean 9-month faculty salary ($)	Estimated change in 9-month average faculty salary for each $100 change in market price ($)
Private Not-for-Profit	0.67	14,926	64,289	19
Public Four-Year	0.45	7,381	71,537	10
Public Two-Year	0.12	2,898	57,833	(1)

Note: It is our convention to use correlation (r) to measure association in a two-variable relationship and R-squared to measure the model's explanatory power in multivariable models.

*These numbers may differ from the mean market price in other tables, based on records omitted for missing faculty salary data.

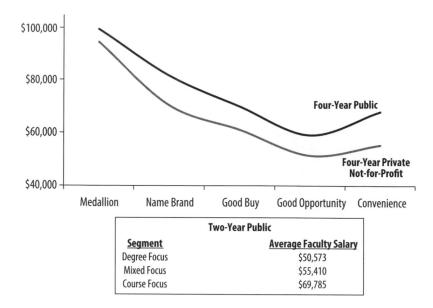

Figure 6.1. Average faculty salaries, by sector and segment

Figure 6.1 displays mean nine-month salaries for full-time faculty, according to the various sectors and segments. The lines in the Four-Year sectors follow the familiar patterns, sloping downward from left to right. On average, faculty at Public colleges and universities are better paid than their counterparts at Private Not-for-Profit ones, except at the upper end of the market, in the Medallion universities. The Private Not-for-Profit sector includes a large number of small liberal arts colleges, and many of them cannot support the salaries found at Public institutions, which often are unionized. In the Two-Year Public sector, as expected, mean salaries in the Degree Focus and Mixed Focus segments align with the Good Opportunity part of the Four-Year market structure, and the Course Focus segment with the Convenience one. The big differences—and they are truly substantial—are not between sectors, but rather across segments. Notably, among Private Not-for-Profit institutions, the mean faculty salary in the Medallion segment is 82 percent higher than the mean in the Good Opportunity portion; the parallel differential in the Public sector is 68 percent.

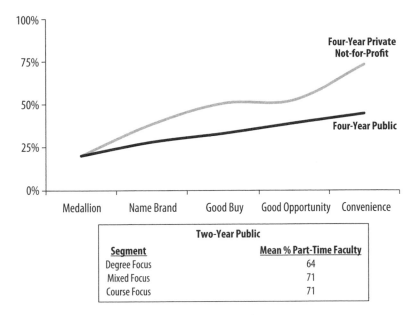

Figure 6.2. Percentages of part-time instructors, by sector and segment

A major concern over the last several decades has been a dramatic increase in the number of part-time faculty—and that, too, tracks with the market. Part-time instructors—often adjunct faculty who are neither on a tenure track nor well paid for their work—are now the norm in the Four-Year Private Not-for-Profit institutions' Good Opportunity and Convenience segments. The number of part-time instructors is slightly less in the Four-Year Public sector, but nonetheless is substantial. Only the Medallion and Name Brand segments in the Public sector and the Medallion one alone in the Private Not-for-Profit sector have proven to be more resistant to the shift to part-time instructors (figure 6.2). Put another way, beyond its top end, today's market for undergraduate education has both allowed and forced institutions to drift away from the ideal of having a faculty principally composed of full-time scholars and teachers. Among the nation's community colleges, there is little variation among segments in the percentage of part-time instructors they employ. In the Two-Year Public sector, as in the Convenience segment of the Private Not-for-Profit sector, the majority of institutions employ armies of part-time instructors.

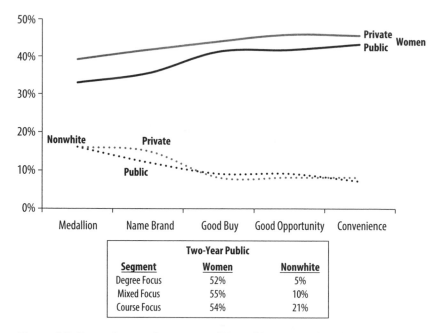

Figure 6.3. Percentages of women and Nonwhite tenured and tenure-track faculty. *Note*: Public=Four-Year Public; Private=Four-Year Private Not-for-Profit.

The market structure laid out in chapter 1 similarly helps explain the demographics of full-time tenured or tenure-track faculty at the nation's colleges and universities. Here, we examine the impact of market segment on four of the populations generally defined as underrepresented within the ranks of tenured and tenure-track faculty: women, Asian, Black (sometimes categorized as "Black or African American"), and Hispanic. We begin with figure 6.3, a composite graph showing the proportion of women and Nonwhites (we apply this term to the three underrepresented minorities identified above) among tenured and tenure-track faculty. What is most striking are the slopes (from left to right) of the solid lines, indicating that women faculty are more likely to be found at less expensive, less selective institutions, regardless of sector. The bias for making male faculty appointments is strongest in the Medallion segment, and, to a slightly lesser extent, in the Name Brand part of the Public Four-Year sector. Notice, however, that across all segments, the median proportion of women is greater in the Private sector than the Public sector.

The dashed lines tell a different story for Nonwhite faculty at Four-Year institutions. They show that the Public and Private sectors are intertwined and are nearly identical. The slope of the dashed lines, particularly from the Medallion to the Good Buy segments, shows that the high-priced, selective part of the market is somewhat more welcoming to minorities (writ large) than the less selective end—the opposite of our finding for women faculty.

The Two-Year Public sector is the only one in which the majority of faculty members are women, and the differences across segments are negligible. The presence of Nonwhite faculty is a different matter. Segment plays a strong role. The median percentage ranges widely from the Degree Focus portion, where Nonwhite faculty make up only 5 percent, to the Course Focus one, where more than one-fifth (21 percent) of the faculty is minority. Looking across the entirety of Public and Not-for-Profit higher education in America, the institutional categories where you are most likely to find a concentration of women or members of underrepresented minorities are in the segment and the sector that is least expensive and least engaged in awarding degrees at either the associate's or bachelor's level. What figure 6.3 makes abundantly obvious is that talking about Nonwhite tenured and tenure-track faculty in general makes as little sense as does assuming that the distribution of faculty members of color is independent of the structure of the market.

When faculty of color are disaggregated in terms of their specific ethnicities, a clearer picture emerges. For the Four-Year institutions, both Private Not-for-Profit and Public, Asians are the dominant Nonwhite ethnic group. Among the Two-Year Public colleges, particularly among the lower-priced, less traditionally academic institutions, the dominant group is Hispanic. While Black or African American faculty continue to play a minor role across all three sectors, they outnumber Hispanics in the Public Four-Year sector.

Figure 6.4 displays the sectors and segments where those who identify themselves as Asian predominate within the group of Nonwhite faculty. Asian faculty members compose about 60 percent of the underrepresented minority faculty in Medallion institutions, and over half of the Nonwhite faculty in Name Brand colleges and universities. Asian faculty constitute a similar percentage in the Good Buy segment of the Public sector. Also, in every segment, they are more prevalent in the Public sector than the Private one.

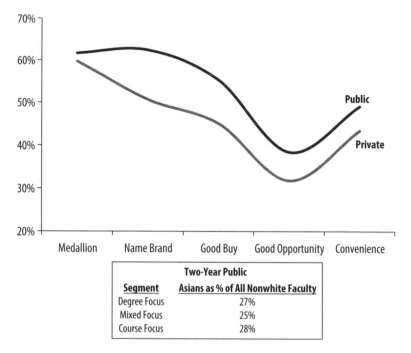

Figure 6.4. Asian faculty, as a percentage of Nonwhite faculty. *Note*: Public=
Four-Year Public; Private=Four-Year Private Not-for-Profit.

Heading for Home

The bottom line is that faculty members are not sufficiently aware
of or interested in the structure or the mechanics of the market that deliv-
ers the undergraduates they teach. Faculty view talking about the market
as disheartening, principally because such conversations inherently de-
value what makes the academy both special and important. Most faculty
fundamentally believe that what ails higher education most is, on the
one hand, the commercialization of the enterprise, and, on the other, a
growing reliance on job-centric metrics to calculate the value of a college
education.

Like policy makers and their policy wonk allies, faculty too often are
the victims of their own ignorance—or, if that is too strong a conclusion,
of their refusal to take the market seriously. What they demand of those
who manage their institutions is often not just unreasonable, but, more
importantly, impractical as well. It is increasingly unlikely in this era of

market competition that college and university administrators can deliver the kinds of students most faculty want to teach. Our colleague Joan Girgus, former dean of the College at Princeton University and former chair of its Psychology Department, occasionally reminds faculty colleagues that our problem is wanting our students to be like us: driven, inherently curious, willing to accept the discipline necessary for scholarly research, and ready to suspend judgment on issues and concerns where there is insufficient evidence to render an informed opinion. Now and for the foreseeable future, at least, students in the age of the Internet are not likely to behave in the same way as faculty members, while the nature of the market for an undergraduate education will increasingly empower them to seek out exactly what they want, whether the faculty likes it or not.

The larger problem, however, is that most scholars are intellectual absolutists. No matter how often we celebrate the virtues of ambiguity in our writings, or couch our findings in the language of probabilities, most of us believe that there are right and wrong answers, good and bad explanations, and satisfactory and unsatisfactory theories. Faculty often speak of the importance of rigor, which includes a willingness to stick with one's intellectual principles through thick and thin.

Put more broadly, most faculty members become noticeably uncomfortable with the workings of educational markets that, in their eyes, diminish the academy by substituting short-term financial goals for time-tested standards that have protected faculty interests and purposes. Historically, faculty dialogues have been about absolutes: the right kind of education, the proper standards for scholarship, the correct way of organizing the academic enterprise. Markets, on the other hand, stress not just competition, but also flexibility and adaptability, and they give only a begrudging advantage to those who maintain their principles to the bitter end.

The antithesis of what most faculty want is something like the market for airline travel that has emerged over the last two decades, in which there are no set prices for any seat on any aircraft before it takes off. Rather, the cost of a ticket is a function of when it was purchased and how willing the traveler was to pay for the small things the airlines now charge extra for. Most carriers today have what they call a load manager, who is in charge of filling the seats on a given flight in such a way as to maximize the revenue that flight produces. If demand is light and the flight is close to departure, the load manager can order a reduction in the ticket price.

To a remarkable degree, that is how college educations are now priced, particularly in the Private Not-for-Profit sector, where discounting has become the norm. The person responsible for assembling the entering class is not called a load manager, but rather a dean of admissions, a dean of financial aid, or a vice president for enrollment management. As summer wanes and "unfilled seats" remain in the freshman class or the transfer cohort, an institution usually becomes more willing to change not its sticker price, but its discounted price. If they could, no doubt these enrollment managers would adjust the product mix as well, accepting extra students into high-demand majors and programs and letting those areas with diminishing demand continue to dwindle.

At the same time, students and their families, particularly those attending mid-market Private institutions, are becoming more skilled at working this system to their advantage. The label attached to the negotiations that often take place between a college or university and a would-be customer is "dialing for dollars," capturing both the mode and purpose of the ensuing conversation. None of this makes the faculty comfortable—it is a matter of the market producing what they were once expected to ordain. Not surprisingly, faculty members decry the consequences of the discounting that seems to rob them of the necessary resources to deliver the level of instruction and the learning experiences expected of them. At the same time, they assert ever more loudly that it is the faculty, and decidedly not the administration, who ought to determine what, exactly, it is that their college or university is promising to deliver. The problem is that this proclamation is, more often than not, a rearguard action. On most campuses, administrators win the battle to launch new majors that promise to attract additional enrollment. What these officials cannot do is reduce the number of programs that are not competitive. Thus costs increase, even as the revenues from the new programs come online.

There is a different option, however, one in which faculty members learn to ask the kinds of questions leading to curricula that are both mission centered and market smart. This alternative means dropping their insistence on absolutes, as well as being more openly amenable to responding to changing market conditions. It also means finding ways to bolster learning, as well as institutional efficiency—and that requires a new willingness to collect and analyze the data that document what faculty do. Not so coincidentally, this need for concrete information found a prominent place in Henry Rosovsky's final report to the Faculty of Arts and Sciences at Harvard University. Seeking to restore the sense of community and the social contract that made the academy possible, Rosovsky urged his colleagues to construct a faculty database that would show such things, among others, as teaching assignments, course enrollments, and thesis advisement, as well as nonteaching activities (e.g., committee service) and a salary history. Rosovsky called for this database to be retroactive, ongoing, and available to department chairs and deans.

Two decades ago, Rosovsky sought the same broad conversation about faculty purposes and processes that is required today if the academy is to succeed as an academic enterprise. Rosovsky closed his report with a dire reminder to his colleagues: "If the status quo continues entirely without reform, the institution that creates and guarantees our freedom and independence may lose the ability to do so" (Rosovsky 1992, 2B).

7

Knowing the Territory

We have filled the pages of this volume with the contours of the US market for an undergraduate education. It is a market so highly segmented that differences between and among individual institutions are minimized, while difference across the four sectors (and their various segments) have become more pronounced. States matter, though, ironically, what is most often missing at the state level are public policies that promote the quality and durability of a state's higher education system. Prices have risen nearly everywhere. While they have not done so uniformly, a frenzy of discounting has weakened many Private Not-for-Profit colleges, perhaps permanently. Those interested in public policy will tell you that student consumers and their parents ought to hold sway, yet they are not parlaying their buying power into either a more effective or a more efficient system of higher education. Jobs increasingly matter, but what constitutes good job data remains an unanswered—some would say even unanswerable— question, leaving institutions free to make promises they are not likely to be held accountable for.

Persuading colleges and universities to change in this, the second decade of the twenty-first century, also requires knowing how these institutions ought to change—and why. It entails being clear about ends as well as means, along with accepting that across a complex system, one size can never fit all. Finally, successful change means knowing what to preserve and reinforce, as well as having the courage to dispense with what is no longer working or simply is not needed.

The larger truth is that most policy makers, like the faculty they too often disparage, have yet to understand how or why today's markets matter.

Little that has passed for public policy over the last four decades can be said to take into account the nature of the competitive markets that now hold sway over almost all institutions of higher education. There is precious little appreciation among the nation's principal policy makers as to how prices are set or how prestige and advantage are distributed.

Equally disappointing is the limited nature of what has become the policy makers' stock-in-trade when discussing what needs to change. In the last decade, just two core ideas have come to dominate all policy discussions focusing on higher education. The first is that too few students who pursue a baccalaureate degree actually earn a BA or its equivalent. Much is made of the reality that the United States no longer leads the civilized world in terms of college completions—a declining statistic that, for many, helps explain why the income gap, separating those at the top from those in the middle and at the bottom, has widened. Increased college participation and graduation rates ought to solve both problems. Having more people pursue a college education would bolster the importance of a strong, employed middle class, while, at the same time, ensure a constantly expanding supply of college-educated workers who, by dint of their creativity and entrepreneurship, will ensure America's economic hegemony.

The principal goal of public policy thus has become keeping or making a college education more affordable. In part, it is a goal that strives to lower the price of a college degree. It also seeks to ensure that the jobs college graduates obtain have sufficient salaries for them to pay off the student loans that funded their college educations. All kinds of schemes have been put forward to achieve these ends, including punishing individual institutions whose graduates do not obtain gainful employment that matches the skills and training they acquired in college. But most policy initiatives are little more than jawboning exercises, designed to supply student shoppers with better information for choosing a college. The practice has been to hold up to public ridicule colleges and universities with students who can't repay their student loans, those with tuition increases that substantially exceed the underlying rate of inflation, and those with financial balance sheets that put the institution at risk.

In the summer of 2013, President Barack Obama traveled to Buffalo, New York, to announce that he was tired of higher education policy initiatives that went nowhere, of tuition increases that exceeded the rate of inflation, and of an attitude on the part of college and university leaders that they could wait out the president and his administration. In other words, these academic officials could exhibit a willingness to talk without actually promising substantive change. Obama's proposed alternative was a tough-minded college rating system that rewarded the virtuous and punished the wasteful. What the president put forth was an extension of previous ideas embraced in the College Scorecard website, which the Department of Education had launched the preceding year. It was a website chock full of the measures the department believed would steer prospective college students toward institutions that promised realistic outcomes and had prices that made sense.

That part of Obama's alternative proposal fell under the rubric business as usual—providing verifiable consumer information about colleges and universities that were practicing what the president was preaching. What was new was the idea that the *federal government* would rate higher education institutions, giving each a numerical score reflecting their quality and their costs, though it quickly became clear that the surrogate for the former was to be increased completion rates and, for the latter, a willingness to hold the line on tuition increases. And the president wasn't just jawboning. The new ratings system would, if implemented, lead to a major redistribution of a portion of the federal pie intended for students, though just how big a change the president had in mind wasn't clear. Previously, almost all of the federal government's $150 billion in annual financial aid had reached colleges and universities indirectly, through the students enrolled in these institutions, and it did not matter how many of those students graduated or how much debt they incurred. "Under the new proposal," as the *New York Time*'s Tamar Lewin (2013) reported, "students could still attend whatever college they chose, public or private." What was different, and it was a big difference, was that "taxpayer support would shift to higher-ranked schools."

Organized higher education winced at the president's proposal. A wide variety of institutional leaders commented on it, though their message was almost always the same. Obama was right to be concerned about prices and completion, as were academic officials. The problem would arise in the details. Would it really be possible to develop objective measures of institutional quality and price using federal data, which everyone knew were prone to error? As is often the case, the American Council on Education's

Terry Hartle summed up the skepticism that those who lobbied on behalf of higher education hoped to introduce into the debate: "There are all kinds of issues, like deciding how far down the road you are looking, and which institutions are comparable. . . . Ultimately, the concern is that the Department of Education will develop a formula and impose it without adequate consultation, and that's what drives campus administrators nuts" (Lewin 2013).

Two years later, the White House pulled the plug on this college ratings scheme, choosing to announce the retreat during a week that otherwise contained good news for Obama, including two major Supreme Court decisions that went his way. The best summary of what had happened to the higher education proposal, and why, was produced by the Associated Press. The nubbin of the AP roundup was that the president himself was "driving the decision to stick with a ratings system" and, until the bitter end, resisting all attempts by both the industry's lobbyists and a growing number of educational experts not just to scale back, but to abandon the effort altogether. Higher education's opposition had been "swift, vehement and nearly universal . . . warning [that] the project was too complex, too subjective and too dependent on shoddy data to ever work fairly" (Associated Press 2015). When the scheme was finally abandoned, its opponents sweetly claimed a victory. Democratic Representative Michael Capuano of Massachusetts was among those, noting: "Do I think they would have continued if no one had pushed back? Of course I do." The lead lobbyist for the National Association of Independent Colleges and Universities added, "They really did listen on this. . . . The more they looked into it, they realized it wasn't doable."

Speaking at the University of Maryland, Baltimore County (UMBC) just days after the announcement that there would be no federal ratings system, the then secretary of education, Arne Duncan, set out to reframe the issue as one of accountability. What was required, he stated, was a renewed effort to hold colleges and universities accountable—their students demanded it, and the public ought to insist on it. Not only was the American higher education system failing too many students, the secretary proclaimed, but it was handicapping the nation as a whole: "The completion challenge [is] not just hurting far too many individuals, it's costing us as a Nation on an international scale. Even as a degree has become critical in a global economy, America has fallen from first in the world in the college completion rates of our young people to twelfth" (US Department of Education 2015). The secretary then spelled out his take on the issue:

> The simple fact is every hard-working student in this country must have a real opportunity to achieve a meaningful, affordable degree. America's prosperity, our democracy, and our identity as a land of opportunity, depends on it. But to get there, we have to think differently. The idea of the past century that public education goes from kindergarten to high school is over. We must make the shift to a vision of quality education that begins much earlier in preschool and continues through postsecondary success. This Administration has done a lot to help pave the way for progress, but there is a lot of heavy lifting and culture change ahead.

And what of the need for those college ratings? It was left to two veteran operatives to deliver the requisite spin. Noting the Obama administration's pledge to provide more and better consumer information to students, Undersecretary of Education Ted Mitchell observed: "It is anything but a retreat. . . . It's a retooling and, we think, an advance on the original concept." The White House followed suit. James Kvaal, deputy director of the White House's Domestic Policy Council, mused, "We are right where the president wanted us to be in terms of making progress toward his vision" (Associated Press 2015).

But this was *not* exactly where Obama wanted to be, having proclaimed in Buffalo: "I think we should rate colleges based on opportunity—are they helping students from all kinds of backgrounds succeed—and on outcomes, on their value to students and parents" (Associated Press 2015). The problem is that what he had in mind simply wasn't possible—or, to put the matter more bluntly, what the president wanted, and what his Department of Education spent two years and untold dollars trying to develop, wasn't feasible, given the structure of an educational market that principally rewarded institutions for their ability to recruit new first-time students. In a word, Obama, his secretary of education, and the coterie of foundation executives and educational experts they assembled simply didn't know the territory. They didn't understand enough about the functioning of the higher education marketplace to produce a credible policy initiative.

All through the process, Department of Education insiders kept hinting that what they wanted was a ratings system that divided colleges and universities into three basic categories: high performing, medium performing, and low performing. The winners would be the high performers, the losers the low performers, and the real target of the effort would be the great mass of institutions in the middle, which, it was hoped, would move into the high-performing category.

It is certainly possible to construct such a scheme, particularly since the Obama administration had focused most of its attention on just two variables: graduation rates and market prices. What this administration was looking for was a set of institutions with *both* high completion rates and low or moderate market prices. The problem is that almost no college or university achieves both. Why? Because graduation rates and market prices are highly correlated: those schools with the best graduation rates are also those with the highest prices.

Among the nearly 980 Four-Year Private Not-for-Profit colleges and universities for which we have both a market price and a graduation rate, just three institutions scored a double—a high completion rate and a low market price—where they were at or above the 80th percentile in their graduation rate and at or below the 20th percentile in price. Two of these schools are small and specialized. Soka University, with 412 students, was founded in 1987 on the Buddhist principles of peace, human rights, and the sanctity of life. Martin Luther College has 775 students, and an emphasis on teacher education and pastoral preparation for the Wisconsin Evangelical Lutheran Synod. The third school that meets these criteria is Brigham Young University, a religious-affiliated institution with nearly 30,000 students, almost all of whom are members of the Church of Jesus Christ of Latter-Day Saints. The pickings were even slimmer among the Four-Year Public colleges and universities. Just two institutions scored the requisite double: Truman State University in Missouri, a school often cited for educational excellence, and the University of Texas at Dallas.

The same pattern characterized the Four-Year Private For-Profit sector. Only one institution, religiously oriented Bob Jones University, met both criteria, with a completion rate in the top 20 percent for this sector and a market price in the bottom 20 percent. Here, however, a note of caution is in order: more than a quarter of the for-profit institutions for which it was possible to calculate an average market price failed to report six-year graduation rates to IPEDS.

Reframing the Issue

In his address at UMBC in 2015, the then secretary of education rightly sought to reframe the issue, moving away from a discussion of ratings and focusing instead on institutional accountability. He saw the increased demand for a college education by a progressively more diverse population as both a challenge and an opportunity. What was needed, he argued, was a willingness to think differently, which, he believed, would result in three major shifts in how policy makers and institutional leaders thought about what was needed in the future:

- "first, dealing with cost and debt;
- second, focusing much more on outcomes;
- and third, driving desperately-needed innovation" (US Department of Education 2015).

The problem with the former secretary's rhetoric is that, lofty though it was, it still missed the mark. What had somehow escaped the secretary was the realization that he was dealing with a market composed of enterprises, and only initiatives that take into account why and how that market works would yield the reforms he sought. It's not that his three goals are wrong, but that, simply put, he couldn't get there from here, in large part because he didn't know the territory. Take the secretary's focus on prices, though he couched his concern instead in terms of costs. He wanted to roll back the tuition prices charged by institutions, thereby making a college education more affordable. He also wanted to reduce, or even eliminate, student debt, though loan funds are often what allowed the students he was most interested in to purchase the college educations they sought.

But neither rhetoric, nor better consumer information, nor, for that matter, more-stringent governmental regulations are likely to yield lower prices. What the federal government, as well as everyone else currently worried about what an undergraduate education costs, need to remember is that it is the market that sets the price charged by most colleges and universities in general, and, in particular, by Medallion institutions. The run-ups in college tuitions Duncan and others so persistently have decried are the prices Medallion institutions find themselves able to charge. Those escalating prices, in turn, are a direct function of the accelerating demand for a place in the freshman class of a Medallion college or university.

Look, for example, at the eight members of the Ivy League group—Medallions all, with hefty endowments, plush campuses, and ever-growing applicant pools. On average, applications to these institutions increased by 82 percent between 2003 and 2013. The average size of their freshman classes, however, increased by just 5 percent. That differential alone is enough to account for their increased prices. To fully understand the nature of this market for highly selective undergraduate institutions, it helps to do the calculation from a student shopper's perspective. In 2003, an individual applying to one of the Ivies had, on average, a one in six chance of being admitted. Ten years later, the probability of admission was less than one in ten. And still they applied in droves.

The problems—and, ultimately, their solutions—differ dramatically across the market. In the Private, elite end of the market, the dysfunctional—and sometimes toxic—nature of its competitive and affluent culture is of great concern. The next tier is stressed by financial pressures that result from the discounting required to secure the most academically able students. The large middle market suffers from unpredictable enrollments, financial uncertainties, and insufficient resources to make the changes needed to stabilize these institutions. The various segments in the Public sector face similar difficulties, with additional pressures from the vagaries of state politics and reduced public funding. The Two-Year sector is home to both the most underresourced institutions, serving the most underresourced students.

Top-Market Perfectionism

In the Medallion segment (and, occasionally, Name Brand), the result is not just much higher prices, but, more importantly, an often unhealthy market for students interested in attending a highly selective college or university. The problem most commentators and policy makers have either ignored or missed is that the schools at the very top of the market—the Ivies, along with the other members of the Consortium on Financing Higher Education and a handful of other high-priced, highly selective institutions—have become increasingly filled with students who are very bright, extremely disciplined, and, much more often than not, from families that are particularly well-off financially. A good measure of the affluence of a student body is the number of "full-pays"—that is, first-time, full-time students not requiring any institutional aid in order to attend that college or university. The average for all eight Ivies was 37 percent, which meant that in 2013 (the most recent year for which IPEDS data were available), more than one out of every three Ivy League students had come from a household that could, on average, afford to pay more than $43,000 per year in tuition alone. It was also the schools in this segment of the market that most consistently increased their sticker prices (i.e., what full-pay students are expected to ante up), on average just under 4 percent per year between 2008 and 2013, while the underlying rate of inflation was only 1.15 percent per year. Those Ivy students who needed monetary assistance received some financial aid, but not a lot, from their enrolling institution. It's hard not to draw the conclusion that these colleges and universities are really filled with kids from families that are well off—or, in the jargon of the day, are rich kids. These rich kids are accustomed to doing exceedingly well in their studies, which is how they gained admission to an Ivy League school.

One of the changes drawing the most comment at these top-of-the-market institutions had been grade inflation, by which is traditionally meant the awarding of too many As and A minuses. In 2004, Princeton University addressed the issue head on, having first, as is the tradition at Princeton, appointed a high-level faculty committee to sort out the facts and then issue a report that includes the necessary changes needed in both practice and policy. What Princeton learned was that yes, giving As had become rampant, with the result that among the seniors graduating in 2002, less than 5 percent had a cumulative grade point average (GPA) that fell below a B minus. As the dean at the time pointed out, "a student with a straight C average . . . stood second to last" in that spring's graduating class (Arenson 2004). The committee's report, in turn, led to a fundamental revamping of Princeton's grading policy, such that, on average, across the university, As would account for only 35 percent of the grades given.

That, by and large, is what the faculty agreed to and delivered. By 2014, when another faculty committee reported on what had come to be known as "grade deflation" at Princeton, the average cumulative GPA of its students had dropped from just over 3.35 in 2002 to well under 3.3 in 2006, only to rise to slightly more than 3.3 in 2013. This upswing in the cumulative GPAs after 2006 elicited fundamental questions about the efficacy, as well as the fairness, of the grade deflation policy the faculty had adopted a decade earlier. The result was another change in Princeton's grading policy. Gone were the limits on As. In their report recommending an end to grade deflation, the committee assembled a variety of evidence as to why a change was necessary. By far the most insightful were the comments from students and others as to the kind of climate that was taking hold at Princeton.

Two of the statements struck us as particularly revealing about how competitive admissions and limited places for entering students yield a culture of conflict and risk, more than is either desirable or healthy. The first of these comments testified to what particularly worried Princeton students: the fairness of the grading process when it was contorted to accommodate the artificial grading restrictions. The second addressed the consequences of grade competition—particularly diminishing collaboration, and even sabotage—in an era of grade deflation: "Classes here often feel like shark tanks" (Princeton University 2014, 12).

The best summation of the impact grade deflation had on the Princeton student body was supplied by chemistry professor Michael Hecht, who described the campus as "a pressure cooker" and suggested that the grading policy had "kept the lid on tight." He continued: "I believe that student well-being, enthusiasm, and peace of mind are important. I would rather our students be motivated by love of learning than anxiety about grades. [The] current grading policy is detrimental to the learning experience and to the campus environment in general" (Princeton University 2014, 13–14).

Just down the road and across the river, the University of Pennsylvania was coping with a different set of lessons about life in a student pressure cooker. In a long, thoughtful essay in the *New York Times*, Julie Scelfo used a report of six student deaths at Penn over a period of 13 months to write frankly about "Suicide on Campus and the Pressure of Perfection" (2015). Her essay weaves together the experiences of two Penn women students, one who committed suicide and another who almost did. As described by Scelfo, Kathryn DeWitt conquered high school like a gold-medal decathlete. When she got to Penn, she discovered that she was "surrounded by people with seemingly greater drive and ability" and "had her first taste of self-doubt." She perceived her classmates as being more accomplished, attractive, and socially adept than she was. Their lives were glamorous and exciting, while hers seemed to be a grind.

Then she learned that Madison Holleran, another Penn freshman, had jumped to her death. Scelfo picked up the story from there. "Ms. DeWitt was stunned. She had never met Ms. Holleran, but she knew the student was popular, attractive and talented. In a blog post . . . Ms. DeWitt would write: 'What the hell, girl?! I was supposed to be the one who went first! You had so much to live for!' Kathryn DeWitt would come frighteningly close to joining her." Scelfo's larger purpose was to ask, as others have and as we are now doing, "Is this highly competitive market for college admissions fundamentally unhealthy?"

> America's culture of hyper achievement among the affluent has been under scrutiny for at least the last decade, but recent suicide clusters, including the deaths of three high school students and one recent graduate in Palo Alto, Calif., have renewed the debate. . . . These cultural dynamics of perfectionism and overindulgence have now combined to create adolescents who are ultra-focused on success but don't know how to fail. (Scelfo 2015)

As we were coming to understand how these same dynamics of perfectionism were playing out during Princeton's discussion of grade deflation, we asked ourselves, "Why should anybody be surprised by all of this?" Our guess is that collectively, a Princeton or Penn entering freshman class is filled by students having straight A high school records—in many cases a necessary but not a sufficient condition to win them a place in either university. Why, then, shouldn't Princeton's grading policy be "the more As the better," since that is the kind of grade the university's students had grown to expect? The Kathryn DeWitt story contained an important aspect of this notion that everyone needs to succeed—to be perfect, really—all of the time. One of the events that unhinged Kathryn during her first semester at Penn was a score in the low 60s she received on her calculus midterm. She believed she had all but failed the test, and perhaps the course, dooming her plan to major in mathematics and become a teacher. Her score was actually good enough to earn an A−, though she simply didn't believe it at the time.

Anthony L. Rostain, a pediatric psychiatrist on Penn's faculty and chair of the task force focusing on the underlying causes of the university's suicide cluster, provided the most succinct summary of what troubles us most about the consequences of an overly competitive admissions market:

"Shame is the sense one has of being defective or, said another way, not good enough. . . . It isn't that one isn't doing well. It's that 'I am no good.' Instead of thinking 'I failed at something,' these students think, 'I am a failure'" (Scelfo 2015).

Mid-Market Madness

Mid-market institutions—principally those we have identified as Good Buy and Good Opportunity colleges and universities—are no more tranquil, but for quite different reasons. For the Four-Year Private Not-for-Profit sector, the past decade has been a rollercoaster ride—ups, downs, twists, near accidents, and, in a few cases, real near-death experiences. The cause of this anxiety has not been dwindling enrollments per se, but rather the constant threat that "this year will be the one in which the bottom falls out of the market."

As it turns out, applications to these colleges and universities have nearly doubled, and that just adds to the chaos. Previously, the first statistic to watch in the annual reading of an institution's changing market position was the number of students who were seeking admission. The problem now is that the unduplicated count of applicants has risen, on average by 8 to 11 percent over the last 10 years. But what has gone up so much faster is the overall number of applications filed by each individual student, an increase occasioned by the mid-market institutions' greater willingness to be part of the "common application process," as well as their growing tendency to wave an application fee. Where a mid-market college typically might have received 1,250 applications for a class of less than 350 freshman plus transfers in 2003, 10 years later it would have 2,200 applications for a class of just under 400 new students. Some institutions tried to fight through the confusion by, in effect, requiring two applications: the first, which was treated primarily as a signal of interest, and, the second, which became the official application. What these colleges and universities have learned in the process is that the only truly reliable indicator of possible enrollment was a potential student's campus visit—and even then, no numbers in early fall seem to provide much assurance of a successful spring. We have worked with a variety of mid-market institutions, and what bothers them most are the wild swings in the market. It is possible to have 380 students in one fall entering class,

310 the next year, and up to 420 the next, before dropping to 335 the following year.

But it is not just the flow of students that seems to defy prediction. More schools in the Good Buy and Good Opportunity segments have preserved their enrollments, only to see the problem transform itself into one of revenue. We have already focused on the chaotic nature of the market prices charged by these colleges and universities, resulting from what is referred to as deep discounting (holding the sticker price constant, or even raising it a little, while simultaneously increasing the amount of institutional financial aid awarded to enrollees). There is a constant scramble for funds, which drains the energy as well as the optimism of an institution.

Beckie Supiano's *Chronicle of Higher Education* story on the annual report by the National Association of College and University Business Officers summed up what most mid-market leaders knew all too well: "All in all, it's not a pretty picture for private colleges. And workable solutions are hard to come by" (Supiano 2015). As she then noted, the report closed on a worried note, stating that "any continuation of the lower enrollments and declines in net tuition and fee dollars seen in the 2014 data could bring even greater challenges to many four-year independent colleges and universities."

Talk to college and university presidents from these market segments, and two laments come to the fore. The first is that planning and investment become the first casualties of a market where the consequences have become increasingly difficult to understand. What these institutional leaders know is that they are in what management gurus call "white water." Turbulence has become the exhausting norm. These presidents are willing to try almost anything: additional programs, a shift in consultants, revised admissions materials, and new admissions personnel (with inflated titles). What they are not able to do is get ahead of the game. They cannot reduce costs fast enough to give them sufficient working capital to change the curriculum, though they have little doubt that better curricular coherence would yield greater efficiencies. It is the *how* that escapes them.

Their second lament is that they have, in fact, become their institutions' chief enrollment officers. They make reports to their respective boards, a process that requires them to confront the impossible: predicting

Table 7.1. Changes in state appropriations (2003–13) in Public mid-market institutions (%)

Sector	33rd percentile	Median	67th percentile
Good Buy	−7%	6%	18%
Good Opportunity	1%	11%	18%

with any certainty the number of students their particular college or university will enroll the next year and, just as importantly, the total net revenue those students will supply. Out of a sense of self-defense, these presidents have become micromanagers: checking all the numbers; gauging the success of specific recruiting events; and making a final decision, often on an ad hoc basis, as to what the institution's forthcoming market price needs to be. Moreover, they do all of this annually, since no one has much faith that the past year's prediction rubrics will continue to hold true in the coming year, let alone for the next couple of years.

Mid-market Four-Year Public colleges and universities are conflicted for other reasons, and in different ways. Like their Private Not-for-Profit counterparts, Four-Year Public Good Buy and Good Opportunity institutions have mostly held their own in the competition for new students. Two-thirds of them had robust increases in the size of their first-year classes. The bottom of the market, however, experienced serious erosion, with one-third of the Good Opportunity schools reporting worrisome declines (upward of 55 students), and 10 percent of all mid-market colleges and universities seeing drops in first-year enrollments that exceeded 220 students.

What distresses these institutions the most, however, is what happens in their respective state legislatures. What Governor Walker aggressively pursued in Wisconsin—a continued freeze on tuition and a $250 million reduction in state funds for the University of Wisconsin System—was harsher than most state policies. Nonetheless, they all are of a kind. Between 2003 and 2013, fully one-third of the Public sector's Good Opportunity and Good Buy institutions had flat or reduced state appropriations (table 7.1). To some extent, Good Buy colleges and universities were able to make up some of their lost revenue by enrolling more first-year and transfer students, a strategy available to fewer of their Good Opportunity counterparts.

Strapped for revenue, these are the institutions that bear the brunt of the criticism for low graduation rates. Across these Public mid-market colleges and universities, the mean six-year graduation rate for the Good Buy institutions was 51 percent, and 33 percent for the Good Opportunity ones. When policy makers and their consultants talk about changing the attainment patterns, these are the schools they have in mind. Not surprisingly, presidents at these colleges and universities feel like they are being targeted for failures that are not of their own or their institution's making. They note, often quite pointedly, that theirs are underresourced schools, serving the bulk of the nation's financially strapped students attending baccalaureate institutions.

These colleges and universities also face an additional problem. Many have faculty unions that have been fiercely successful at preserving the rights and privileges—along with the economic well-being—of their members, despite the stinginess of many state legislatures and, in a growing number of states, the outright hostility of Republican legislative majorities. From a union perspective, curricular reform requires significant work-rule changes, and those must be negotiated. The difficulty is that the administrations of these mid-market Public institutions have little to bargain with: they can't hire more faculty; they can't change teaching loads, since the legislature is looking over their shoulders; and they can't reduce the number of either courses or majors, though that result might well yield a more efficient as well as a more effective curriculum. What they can do— and frequently try to accomplish—is increase the number of adjunct faculty, on the one hand, and, on the other, open new programs in search of additional enrollments. No one should be surprised that in the wake of state-imposed restrictions, the University of Wisconsin–Eau Claire reengineered its administrative structure but largely left its faculty and their educational functions untouched.

The irony, of course, is that these mid-market colleges and universities hold the key to a successful reformation of the American system of higher education. The big changes sought by the federal government and most policy wonks need to happen here, if there is a chance for a real increase in the number of students completing their college education. The problem, to repeat our earlier observation, is that Four-Year mid-market institutions and, often, the students they serve are equally needy. No matter how soaring the rhetoric, with no substantive additions to the resources available to these institutions and their students, little change is likely.

Base-Market Compaction

An even larger share of financially strapped students enroll in schools in the Two-Year Public sector. In 2012, out of the 6.5 million Pell Grant recipients included in our IPEDS database, 3 million, or just under half (48 percent), attended a Two-Year Public institution. The Four-Year Private For-Profit sector also has large numbers of Pell Grant recipients, but it enrolls a smaller proportion of the nation's undergraduate population. What figure 7.1 makes clear is just how little has changed in almost 50 years, when *The Academic Revolution* noted that those students who were the toughest to teach were crowded into the institutions with the fewest resources per student (Jenks and Riesman 1968). On average, among the more than 1,000 Two-Year Publics for which there were sufficient data to be included in our market segment model, 40 percent of their full-time enrollees were Pell recipients. Only the Four-Year Private For-Profit segment had a higher proportion of Pell recipients (55 percent).

Two-Year Public institutions come in all shapes and sizes. A few are mega-systems, with upward of 50,000 students. Miami Dade College and Indiana's Ivy Tech Community College System are two examples: the former with more than 65,000 undergraduates in the fall of 2013, and the latter with just under 100,000. And some of them are remarkably small— that same fall, one-third of all the Two-Year Publics in our analysis had enrollments of less than 2,500. Most schools in this sector were equally welcoming to full- and part-time students. For the entire set of 1,006 Two-Year institutions reporting data in 2013, the median percentage of full-time students was 58, practically unchanged since 2003. But there had been shifts over that decade, some of them quite dramatic. A third of the colleges in the Two-Year Public sector had enrollment growths exceeding 25 percent, and the median increase was 13 percent. Twenty percent of these schools lost some enrollment, while the bottom 10 percent suffered declines of 20 percent or more.

In the Two-Year Public sector, as in the Four-Year Public one, there were winners and losers in the quest for public funds to operate their campuses. Roughly 40 percent of the Two-Year schools suffered declines in their total operating revenues, though comparisons are difficult to make,

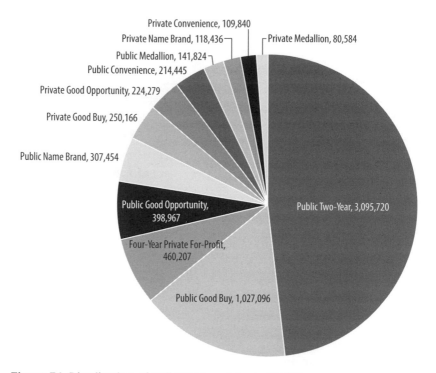

Figure 7.1. Distribution of Pell Grant recipients (2012)

in part because the Two-Year Publics were less diligent in reporting their 2003 operating revenues, as well as because there were changes in accounting procedures across the sector. What is clear, however, is that, with few exceptions, these institutions continued to be the most underresourced in the industry.

The Two-Year Public sector is changing in ways hardly imagined in the past century. The term "community college" is becoming an anachronism. The sector's primary degree remains an associate's degree, but most of these institutions are now in the credentialing business, offering certificates for special skills and, in increasing numbers, bachelor's degrees in programs with a specific vocational emphasis. Who attends a community college today? Lots and lots of people, with differing expectations and capacities. Some are purely vocational schools, in the old-fashioned meaning of the word. Others are what might best be called blended institutions, proud of their flexibility to serve almost anyone who wants to be taught.

Although the Two-Year Public sector forms nearly 40 percent of the postsecondary education market, these schools remain the least celebrated and, above all, the least well-funded component of the nation's higher education system. In whatever parsing is done in any reform agenda, the Two-Year Publics must play a central role, though it remains anyone's guess about how to craft a policy initiative that embraces all but a slice of them at any one time. It is not untoward, then, that the current policy buzz involves having Two-Year Public schools with zero or near-zero tuitions, though what these institutions need is not more students, but more venture capital with which to recast their basic operations.

Nor should it be surprising that in the industry as a whole—across the four dominant sectors we have described, along with their principal segments—confusion should reign. It is no longer possible to describe the American system of higher education within a single breath. Its exceptions and peculiarities outnumber its settled principles. Do degrees across the spectrum mean the same thing? Not really. Is it possible to speak of a higher education mission, as the state of Wisconsin once did in propounding the Wisconsin Idea? That is no longer possible, either, as the residents of Wisconsin and those outsiders who once admired the state's former commitment to its higher education system have learned, to their dismay. Where are the grand initiatives that were once the hallmark of the United States' investment in public higher education? They, too, are largely gone. Even the best of them—Clark Kerr's California Master Plan for Higher Education and North Carolina's educational pathway to economic development—are recognized today more as historical footnotes, rather than as signposts teaching a new generation of policy makers and institutional leaders how to excel in an era when market competition, rather than public policy, defines the postsecondary landscape.

Epilogue

What those who would reform, if not actually remake, American higher education now confront is a market landscape that is as tough as it is unforgiving. There are too few resources, too many constituencies expecting to be served, and too little certainty as to what constitutes a quality product. Public institutions, in particular, are being shaped by churlish politicians no longer willing to see higher education as a public good. More generally, there is a new willingness to discount the importance of academic traditions and prerogatives. The result is an environment in which there are many losers and few winners. Even those at the top of the heap—the nation's Medallion institutions, filled with bright, eager students whose parents seem all too willing to pay almost any price to have their children attend a prestigious institution—now wonder if their competitive environments yield successful learners. The base of the market is where the most needy, in almost every sense of the term, enroll in institutions that all too often lack sufficient resources to get the job done. The middle of the market consists of institutions—along with students and their families—that feel trapped by high prices, low returns, and political nostrums of doubtful benefit. From our perspective, there are but three basic propositions that, if fully implemented, hold out a promise of promoting educational reform in an era of pronounced market competition.

Have Teaching Become Group Work

It is way past the time to stop diminishing the clout of traditional faculty, the full-time teacher-scholars who once confidently served as academic stewards of the colleges and universities that appointed them. Here the problem is not just a toxic external environment, but, equally, an internal culture largely unprepared to produce the kind of reforms that are needed. Too often now, those at the top of the market invest more of their personal energies in enterprises that are often tangential to their school's time-honored missions. These faculty engage in research institutes and other big-team research enterprises; in consulting practices and international forays; and in the teaching of their own courses, which they have successfully walled off from those of their colleagues.

In part, their isolation is self-directed, but it is also the case that faculty across the spectrum are being marginalized—by the administrators at their own institutions, by the agency and foundation staffs who think they know better, and by a competitive market they too frequently misunderstand. Faculty see themselves as victims of a wrongheaded notion that education is a commodity, and that colleges and universities have customers who, without knowing the kind of education they really need, complain far too readily that the academic requirements faculty impose, often in support of a general education, are a waste of their time and their money.

It is a frame of mind that makes genuine reform ever more challenging. In many ways, faculty are more inventive than ever—innovations generated by them abound—but their ideas about educational reform are almost never woven into the fabric of their institutions. Part of the problem is that these concepts ultimately prove to be hopelessly expensive. In a recent doctoral dissertation for the University of Pennsylvania's Executive Doctorate in Higher Education Management program, Reyes Gonzalez analyzed two successful, faculty-driven reform efforts: one at a public comprehensive university, and the other at a mid-market liberal arts college. Both achieved the educational goals promised by the leaders of the two efforts, but each set of changes has proven to be problematic, becoming unaffordable for their respective institutions as a whole. In one, the revised curriculum required a substantial increase in the size of the faculty, and in the other, the reform actually contributed to a downturn in enrollments.

That is the reformer's dilemma: how to energize faculty who are increasingly detached and often angry at the role the market has come to play in their lives and their institutions. Presidents, provosts, and deans, not knowing how to solve that problem, have increasingly turned to others—foundation staff, agency officials, consultants—to design curricula that will be more efficient, help attract a shifting student market, and be able to garner the necessary financial resources.

It is not a matter of faculty stubbornness, although there are plenty of recalcitrant faculty on most campuses to make those who propose curricular changes think twice before bringing their efforts to market. As part of a parallel research effort funded by the Teagle Foundation, we have begun collecting such faculty stories, with a particular emphasis on the kinds of obstacles these individuals have encountered when pursuing curricular reform. Real difficulties occur when innovations the faculty want to put in place come up against the rules of the game that define teaching loads, the processes by which new courses and majors are approved, and the requirements faculty members themselves have imposed for graduation. Our conclusion: curricular, and, hence, institutional, reforms require substantive rule changes that must be put in place at the same time as the new curricula are introduced. The most important is to cease treating each member of the faculty as an independent agent or contractor, responsible just for his or her own teaching. Teaching must once again become group work, in which the department or program becomes a kind of learning cooperative, where tasks and responsibilities are shared. Amending the work rules that define faculty effort is now a necessary condition for changing the curriculum, which, in turn, is a requirement for making colleges and universities more financially efficient.

Provide Direct Appropriations and Operating Subsidies to Colleges and Universities

Those who would recast America's higher education system have much to learn from those who seek to reshape the nation's energy markets. To encourage the use of renewable forms of energy, they do not rely on the market itself to produce the innovations that achieving a more sustainable system requires. Instead, most public policies in pursuit of that goal are a mix of regulations, tax incentives, and direct investment in the companies and other entities the government believes will be responsible for the concepts and products that, in time, will first come to scale and then become supported by a domestic energy market.

If public officials want higher education reforms that provide enhanced quality and greater innovation, they will have to be similarly willing to pay for the changes they seek. They will also have to be creative in putting rules and incentives in place that will govern the distribution of the funds they appropriate. Moreover, they will have to think carefully about the effects of providing direct—and substantially augmented—investments to the nation's colleges and universities.

It is also worth noting that the federal government already makes sizeable direct investments in a limited number of universities, through grants and contracts from the National Institutes of Health (NIH), the National Science Foundation (NSF), the Department of Defense (DOD), and the Department of Energy (DOE—not to be confused with the Department of Education). The sums are significant: $23-plus billion per year for the NIH; $5.2 billion for the NSF; $4.4 billion to academic institutions from the DOE; and a lesser, though still substantial amount, from the DOD. The federal government operates a regulated market in which institutions and other entities compete with each other for sponsored awards. In these funding agencies, panels composed of peers review the grant and contract applications, while specialized federal auditors are responsible for the complex rules governing the payment of direct expenditures and the reimbursement of allowable indirect costs.

A similarly regulated but more broadly based market, with the same kinds of rules for direct expenditures and allowable indirect costs, needs to become a political possibility in higher education. Three content domains would greatly benefit from federally supplied research and development funds. The first is science, technology, engineering, and mathematics (STEM) education. Much of this funding would probably flow to institutions at the top of the market, given their prior investments in STEM education. The second would be instructional technology, speeding the process of integrating new electronic devices and formats, as well as and social media applications, into the world of learning. This effort needs to be truly faculty guided. Just as importantly, it must become student centric. A significant portion of these funds should be earmarked for mid-market institutions— colleges and universities employing those with substantial talents, but without enough funds (at their current market prices) to develop, test, and then implement new modes of instruction. The third would be remedial education—not its actual delivery, but rather the testing and validation of new ways to make more students both college ready and college successful.

Beyond these funds for research and development, there is an equal, perhaps even more compelling need to provide direct support to institutions at the base of the higher education market. Of the myriad lessons we have drawn from our analysis of this market in the United States, the most dismaying is the maldistribution of resources across the system. Here, the market has clearly worked against the nation's stated goals of providing quality postsecondary education, at a reasonable price, to an ever-expanding percentage of America's adult population. Instead, the rich—both institutions and student families—have gotten richer and the poor, too often, have been forgotten.

Thus our second proposition includes a call to appropriate direct operating subsidies for those colleges and universities responsible for enrolling the largest number of underresourced students. In the 1960s, the federal government put student aid programs in place, giving direct support to students through loans and grants. Since then, the market has been ascendant. Students are expected to vote with their feet, choosing for themselves the best institutions to attend at a price they can afford to pay, with help from the federal government in the form of Pell Grants and subsidized loans. Over the last four-plus decades, those programs have helped underwrite a substantial increase in the number and proportion of Americans who seek a postsecondary education. But, in addition to having a sizeable price tag, it is an achievement that has produced uneven results.

Our data analyses have persuaded us that the United States will not achieve its stated educational goals as long as students with the greatest needs are enrolled in the nation's most underresourced colleges and universities. The deficits among this population and this set of institutions are well recognized, but once again the proposed solution—making community colleges tuition free—is hardly market smart. Reducing the cost of attendance for these schools may make sense politically, and it would probably be a boon to the most economically disadvantaged members of the student body, but it does not make sense educationally. What institutions that enroll this population need are not lower prices, but—to put the matter baldly—more money. The $60 billion that a zero or near-zero tuition program would cost the federal treasury would be much better spent providing smaller classes, cohort-based curricula options, and more-intensive advising in the schools where these students are most likely to enroll.

We well understand the pitfalls that can accompany federal operating subsidies: a loss of local control, extraordinary opportunities for political mischief when deciding which institutions receive the subsidies, and an equally disabling possibility that corrupt practices will accompany poorly audited disbursements. The alternative to direct investment in those schools that enroll the majority of underresourced students, however, seems to be more of the same—a greater focus on price, rather than on the educational process. On the one hand, this latter approach would produce more churning, as students pass in and out of a variety of institutions. On the other, it would not foster a real improvement in the rate at which such students graduate from an accredited college or university.

Understand How Higher Education Can and Cannot Promote Economic Growth

Then there are the temptations that need to be resisted. Principal among them is the urge to promise an era of individual and community prosperity as the reward for greater state appropriations for colleges and universities. Institutional leaders have been more than willing to pledge what they ought to know higher education cannot deliver. Perhaps the most dangerous belief of all is the one that stills holds sway: if colleges and universities educate and train more people, these individuals will find the jobs they need to pay back the loans they took out to pay for their college educations. Jobs will not magically appear in those states that invest more in their postsecondary institutions.

The question that looms over the discussion of jobs, and a higher education market that has become more vocational, is the one Peter Cappelli (2015) asks in the title of his recent book, *Will College Pay Off?* If current data documenting the labor market experiences of recent college graduates can be relied on, the answer is yes, for about two-thirds of them. They will accept jobs, at decent rates of pay, that do take good advantage of the college degrees they have just acquired. The remaining third will probably find employment and have higher earnings than those who did not earn a degree, but whether they will acquire jobs that fully utilize their college educations remains an open question. This much, at least, is clear: a college education does not guarantee entrance into the middle class, particularly for those financially or otherwise disadvantaged students who undertake their studies in an underresourced college or university.

The best discussion of why this underemployment of college graduates is likely to continue, or even accelerate, has been provided by the authors of *The Global Auction: The Broken Promises of Education, Jobs, and Incomes* (Brown, Lauder, and Ashton 2010). The problem, they point out, is that the global supply of college graduates has begun to exceed the demand for their services—an imbalance that most likely will continue for the indefinite future. As a result, the exportation of American knowledge-based jobs will probably increase, following much the same path as the outsourcing of US manufacturing jobs that began more than three decades ago.

The answer, the authors of *The Global Auction* argue, is at least a partial return to the Keynesian economic principles that prevailed in the 1950s and 1960s. In their view, markets will still hold sway, but the role of government will increasingly become one of funding critical enterprises and putting in place regulations and tax policies that minimize the value of short-term investments, forcing all those in the marketplace to reach for longer-term advantages.

What the American economy requires first, Brown, Lauder, and Ashton argue, is not an increase in college graduates per se, but an ever-expanding number of jobs that take advantage of the creative talents those graduates can bring to the labor market. Governmental policies and initiatives, rather than institutional investments, are the proven means for creating new jobs. In other words, first foster the demand for better-trained workers, and then help the entire educational system produce the kinds of employees an expanding economy requires.

There are plenty of American examples from the period just after the Second World War that make our point. The first is the GI Bill, which was conceived as labor policy, rather than educational policy. The assumption was that the nation's postwar economy could not absorb all the returning veterans, who had spent the previous three years in uniform. Sending them to college was viewed as a buffer against massive unemployment, as well as a means of rewarding the country's fighting men and women. Other postwar policies, often Keynesian in nature, helped create the postwar boom that was fulfilled in the GI Bill's learn-to-earn promise.

The second example is the reforms and initiatives put in place by Luther Hodges, Terry Sanford, and Bill Friday in North Carolina. What that state did, which turned out remarkably well, was to create real incentives that encouraged northern companies to move south. One of those factors was a nonunion workforce, but tax incentives and an explicit willingness to invest in the state's educational providers—at every level—were just as important. What North Carolina promised was, "If you come, we will build it."

What we have in mind is a reprise of the bargain implicit in both the GI Bill and the North Carolina Promise—an active understanding by government that job creation requires a true public/private partnership, one that is both mission centered and market smart.

A Final Note

We are aware that our three basic propositions for defining good higher education public policy in an era of market competition assume that it is federal policies that will matter most. Just as it is too late to turn back the clock and abandon the initiatives that made market competition the principal distributor of federal funds in support of students seeking a college education, so, too, is it past the time to expect states to reassert themselves as the principal owners and regulators of the nation's colleges and universities.

At the same time, state governments have made either rolling back or controlling the prices public colleges and universities charge the cornerstone of their state's educational policy. Talk to these legislators, and they will tell you that what they want most are reduced tuitions. Lower prices are what their constituents are asking for, and what politically smart legislators are hell bent on delivering. The biggest obstacles to the kinds of reforms we have advocated have occurred in those states that have sought a fundamental reduction in appropriations to their public colleges and universities. Recall the challenge the University of Wisconsin–Eau Claire faced: a sudden, 22 percent cut in its state appropriation. And remember the university's response—a massive reengineering of administrative functions that left its academic components largely untouched.

We believe that there is an important role for the states to play in an increasingly federalized system of higher education. States will need to continue to certify institutions of higher education within their borders, authorizing them to grant degrees and specifying the kinds of reports they must submit to maintain that certification. A more important role for each state, however, will be to implement the federal government's programmatic initiatives. We simply do not believe the US Department of Education has either the staff or, frankly, the moxie to put into practice the kinds of programs utilizing direct subsidies and investments we have called for. What is required instead is a set of new federal/state partner-ships. The federal government should supply the necessary funds. The states, however, ought to be the initial movers in support of a national program of higher education reform. It is at this level that the know-how for implementing programs that support state-defined values and traditions resides—and it is this sense of local empowerment and interest that will be essential in attaining the ends we have in mind.

In closing, we were reminded of a story that appeared in the *New York Times* at about the same time as President Barack Obama was promoting a system for rating colleges and universities in terms of their affordability, accessibility, and capacity for producing college graduates. "Mr. Obama," the *Times'* Tamar Lewin reported, declared "that tinkering around the edges would not be enough, and that the changes he was proposing . . . 'won't be popular with everyone—including some who've made higher ed-ucation their business—but it's past time that more of our colleges work better for the students they exist to serve'" (Lewin 2013). We agree, but we also believe that in an age of global labor and educational markets, achiev-ing these goals will take greater resolve and more federal funds than the current president of the United States probably imagines.

References

Arenson, Karen W. 2004. "Princeton Tries to Put a Cap on Giving A's." *New York Times*, April 8. www.nytimes.com/2004/04/08/nyregion/princeton-tries-to-put-a-cap-on -giving-a-s.html.

Arum, Richard, and Josipa Roksa. 2011a. *Academically Adrift: Limited Learning on College Campuses*. Chicago, IL: University of Chicago Press.

Arum, Richard, and Josipa Roksa. 2011b. "Your So-Called Education." *New York Times*, May 14. www.nytimes.com/2011/05/15/opinion/15arum.html?scp=2&sq/.

Associated Press. 2015. "How Obama Reversed Course on Federal College Ratings." *New York Times*, July 2. www.msn.com/en-us/news/politics/how-obama-reversed-course -on-federal-college-ratings/ar-AActLos/.

Bauer, Scott. 2015."Wisconsin Gov. Walker Proposes Drug Testing, University Cut." The Big Story, *Associated Press*, February 3. www.dailyherald.com/article/20150203/news /302039704/.

Bowen, William G., Matthew M. Chingos, and Michael S. McPherson. 2011. *Crossing the Finish Line: Completing College at America's Public Universities*. Princeton, NJ: Princeton University Press.

Brown, Phillip, Hugh Lauder, and David Ashton. 2010. *The Global Auction: The Broken Promises of Education, Jobs, and Incomes*. (Kindle edition.) Oxford, UK: Oxford University Press.

Cappelli, Peter. 2015. *Will College Pay Off?: A Guide to the Most Important Financial Decision You'll Ever Make*. New York, NY: Public Affairs.

Carnevale, Anthony P., Ban Cheah, and Andrew R. Hanson. 2015. *The Economic Value of College Majors*. Washington, DC: Center on Education and the Workforce, Georgetown University. https://cew.georgetown.edu/cew-reports/valueofcollegemajors/.

Change. 1998. "The User-Friendly Terrain: Defining the Market Taxonomy for Two-Year Institutions." The Landscape, *Change* 30(1), January/February: 57–60.

Change. 2003. "Best in Show: Rethinking the Rankings Game." The Landscape, *Change* 35(5), September/October: 55–58.

CHE [*Chronicle of Higher Education*]. 2015. "Caught between a Cap on Tuition Increases and Cuts in State Aid." *Chronicle of Higher Education*, July 10. www.chronicle.com/article /caught-between-a-cap-on/231517?cid=at&utm_source=at&utm_medium=en/.

Delbanco, Andrew. 2007. "Academic Business." *New York Times Magazine*, September 30. www.nytimes.com/2007/09/30/magazine/30wwln-lede-t.html?pagewanted =print/.

EPLC [Education Policy and Leadership Center], and TLA [Learning Alliance for Higher Education]. 2006. *A Rising Tide: The Current State of Higher Education in the Commonwealth of Pennsylvania*. April. Harrisburg, PA: EPLC and West Chester, PA: TLA.

Finney, Joni E., and Patrick M. Callan. 2014. "California Must Revise Master Plan for Higher Education." *SF GATE*, August 22. www.sfgate.com/opinion/article/California -must-revise-Master-Plan-for-Higher-5704590.php.

Friedman, Thomas. 2005. *The World Is Flat: A Brief History of the Twenty-First Century*. New York, NY: Farrar, Straus, and Giroux.

Gergen, David. 2017. "Gergen: Trump Swings Wildly at Wrong Target." Opinion, *CNN .COM*, January 13. www.cnn.com/2017/01/11/opinions/donald-trump-news-conference -gergen/.

Glenn, David. 2010. "Scholar Raises Doubts about the Value of a Test of Student Learning." *Chronicle of Higher Education*, June 2. www.chronicle.com/article/Scholar-Raises -Doubts-About/65741/.

Jenks, Christopher, and David Riesman. 1968. *The Academic Revolution*. Garden City, NY: Doubleday.

Lewin, Tamar. 2013. "Obama's Plan Aims to Lower Cost of College." *New York Times*, August 22. www.nytimes.com/2013/08/22/education/obamas-plan-aims-to-lower-cost -of-college.html.

McCormick, Alexander C., and Chun-Mei Zhao. 2005. "Rethinking and Reframing the Carnegie Classification." *Change* 37(5), September/October: 51–57.

NCES [National Center for Education Statistics]. 2010. "CIP 2010: Crosswalk." *Classification of Instructional Programs* (CIP), Integrated Postsecondary Education Data System (IPEDS). https://nces.ed.gov/ipeds/cipcode/crosswalk.aspx?y=55/.

NCPPHE [National Center for Public Policy and Higher Education]. 2000. *Measuring Up 2000: The State-by-State Report Card for Higher Education*. San Jose, CA: National Center for Public Policy and Higher Education.

NCPPHE [National Center for Public Policy and Higher Education]. 2008. *Measuring Up 2008: The National Report Card on Higher Education*. San Jose, CA: National Center for Public Policy and Higher Education.

New, Jake. 2015. "Pedigree." *Inside Higher Ed*, May 27. https://www.insidehighered.com /news/2015/05/27/qa-author-new-book-how-elite-students-get-elite-jobs/.

NILOA [National Institute for Learning Outcomes Assessment]. 2015. "Tests: Collegiate Learning Assessment (CLA)." www.learningoutcomeassessment.org/test_CLA.html [accessed November 17, 2016].

Perna, Laura W., and Joni E. Finney. 2014. *The Attainment Agenda: State Policy Leadership in Higher Education*. Baltimore, MD: Johns Hopkins University Press.

PHERP [Pew Higher Education Research Program]. 1988. "Seeing Straight Through the Muddle." *Policy Perspectives* 1(1), September: 1.

Princeton University. 2014. "Report from the Ad Hoc Committee to Review Policies Regarding Assessment and Grading." August 5. www.princeton.edu/main/news /archive/S40/73/33I92/PU_Grading_Policy_Report_2014_Aug.pdf.

Reisberg, Leo. 2000. "Are Students Actually Learning?" *Chronicle of Higher Education*, November 17. www.chronicle.com/article/Are-Students-Actually/17612/.

Rivera, Lauren. 2015. "Guess Who Doesn't Fit In at Work." Sunday Review: Opinion, *New York Times*. May 30. https://www.nytimes.com/2015/05/31/opinion/sunday/guess-who -doesnt-fit-in-at-work.html?_r=1/.

Roosevelt, Theodore. 1912. "Introduction." In Charles McCarthy, *The Wisconsin Idea*. http://digicoll.library.wisc.edu/WIReader/WER1650-1.html.

Rosovsky, Henry. 1991. "Annual Report of the Dean of the Faculty of Arts and Sciences, 1990–1991." Excerpted in *Policy Perspectives* 4(3), September 1992: section B.

Rothwell, Jonathan, and Siddharth Kulkarni. 2015. *Beyond College Rankings: A Value-Added Approach to Assessing Two- and Four-Year Schools*. Washington, DC: Brookings Institution. www.brookings.edu/research/reports2/2015/04/29-beyond-college-rankings-rothwell-kulkarni#interactive/.

Scelfo, Julie. 2015. "Suicide on Campus and the Pressure of Perfection." *New York Times*, July 27. https://www.nytimes.com/2015/08/02/education/edlife/stress-social-media-and-suicide-on-campus.html.

Shaman, Susan, and Robert Zemsky. 1984. "Perspectives on Pricing." In Larry H. Litten (Ed.), *Issues in Pricing Undergraduate Education*. New Directions for Institutional Research No. 42 (June), 7–18.

Soares, Louis. 2011. "Guiding Innovation in Higher Education." Presentation at Center for American Progress, Washington, DC, June 29. www.americanprogress.org/issues/economy/news/2011/06/29/9868/guiding-innovation-in-higher-education/.

Supiano, Beckie. 2014. "Why Comparing Lots of Colleges Might Not Help as Many Students as You'd Think." *Chronicle of Higher Education*, December 19. http://chronicle.com/article/Why-Comparing-Lots-of-Colleges/150937/.

Supiano, Beckie. 2015. "Tuition Discount Rates Rise Again, Signaling Potential Challenges for Private Colleges." *Chronicle of Higher Education*, August 25. http://chronicle.com/article/Tuition-Discount-Rates-Rise/232579/.

US Department of Education. 2006. *A Test of Leadership: Charting the Future of U.S. Higher Education; A Report of the Commission Appointed by Secretary of Education Margaret Spellings*. Washington, DC: US Department of Education. https://www2.ed.gov/about/bdscomm/list/hiedfuture/reports.html.

US Department of Education. 2015. "Toward a New Focus on Outcomes in Higher Education." Remarks by Secretary of Education Arne Duncan, University of Maryland, Baltimore County (UMBC), July 27. US Department of Education. https://www.ed.gov/news/speeches/toward-new-focus-outcomes-higher-education.

UW–Madison [University of Wisconsin–Madison]. 2017. "The Wisconsin Idea." http://www.wisc.edu/wisconsin-idea/.

Woodhouse, Kellie. 2015. "Struggling to Stay True to Wisconsin's Ideals." *Inside Higher Ed*, July 29. https://www.insidehighered.com/news/2015/07/29/university-wisconsin-eau-claire-responds-massive-cuts-state-support/.

Zemsky, Robert, and Penny Oedel. 1983. *The Structure of College Choice*. Princeton, NJ: College Board.

Zemsky, Robert, Susan Shaman, and Daniel B. Shapiro. 2001. *Higher Education as Competitive Enterprise: When Markets Matter*. New Directions for Institutional Research No. 111 (Fall). San Francisco, CA: Jossey-Bass.

Index